First published in 2004 by the authors
26 Falklands Road, Burnham on Crouch, Essex CM0 8SN
Radway Cottage, Radway, Warwickshire CV35 0UN

© 2004 Carol Cashmore and Tim Smith-Vincent

ISBN 0 9522812 4 4

Front cover:
Policeman, model number 85, 13 inches high, decorated by Susan. Some policemen have just the usual star as the badge on their helmet but other versions, including this one, have Susan's initials SP within the star. In addition the number on this policeman's collar is the 1950's telephone number for The Lodge at Brabourne Lees.

The large dog, Susan's model of her French bulldog, Beetle, model number 19, height 8½ inches.

Back cover:
Three piping women, a rear view of the model illustrated on page 104. 11 inches long 8½ inches high.

Pages 1 and 6: Susan's drawings.

Pages 4 and 5: Row of school girls, model number 52, 10 inches long and 3 inches high.

Susan Parkinson and the Richard Parkinson Pottery

**Carol Cashmore
and
Tim Smith-Vincent**

CONTENTS

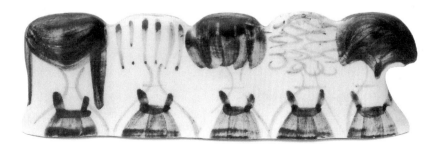

ACKNOWLEDGEMENTS

The impetus for this book arose from the admiration of the work of Susan Parkinson and the desire to know more about the Richard Parkinson Pottery. With Susan's cooperation and patience we have been able to piece together the history of the Pottery. Her involvement made our task much easier and so enjoyable. We are indebted to her for all her support, openness and memories of the Pottery.

Susan introduced us to members of her family, friends and former employees who all helped in the compilation of the book. Their recollections of the Pottery were most enjoyable to listen to and greatly assisted us in building a picture of the Pottery and its ceramics. Their time, support and encouragement are much appreciated.

Lastly we wish to extend our grateful thanks to those collectors of Richard Parkinson Pottery who gave us access to their collections and allowed their models to be photographed for inclusion in the book.

Carol Cashmore

Tim Smith-Vincent

CHAPTER 1   ENTIRELY BY ACCIDENT!

Susan Sanderson

Susan Sanderson was born in India in 1925. Her father worked for the wine merchants Phipson and Co. in Bombay but he was more interested in natural history and cricket than the wine trade. Rather luckily some of the Bombay Natural History Museum's exhibits were temporarily stored in the same building as his office, and when he came to appoint a new employee he would say *'choose the person who is a good bowler'* or whatever position the cricket team needed at the time. Susan's mother's family came from Ireland. Her mother had a very practical bent and enjoyed carpentry as well as the more traditional female skills of embroidery and dressmaking and Susan inherited these abilities, especially her skill at carpentry. As Susan's father worked in India for most of his married life, her mother had some difficult decisions to make regarding the family. It was the common wisdom of the time that children did not fare well in that climate, because of this Susan left India and returned to England when she was just four years old and so she has few memories of her early life in India. Her mother spent many years alternating between the two countries, probably spending more time in Britain than India.

Susan and her mother lived in Buckinghamshire when they first returned to England before settling permanently in Tenterden, Kent. Susan went to a small private boarding school, called Maltman's Green at Gerrards Cross, which she considered quite unique. It had about 60 pupils and Susan described it as *'a one person school'* as it relied on, and seemed to be entirely run by, the Head Mistress. Susan remembered the Head Mistress as *'a remarkable but terrifying character'* who kept everyone well under control. *'She was the sort of person who knew precisely what was going on behind her back in the next room'*. Susan thought that most of the pupils probably ended up with fearful inferiority complexes as a result. Maltman's Green had many extra-curricula activities, including a pottery room, and was particularly good at producing talented artists and actors. Susan's sister, Diana, who was 7 years her elder, had gone to the same school and on leaving went to the Webber Douglas Academy of Dramatic Art in Kensington, London. But she remained there for only one year before leaving to spend nearly two years in India with her father.

Top of the page: The unicorn decorated with fleur de lys. Model number 3, 6¾ inches high. A crack can just be seen at the top of the neck on this model. In the collection of Barbara McAdam-Seth.

Susan left Maltman's Green when she was only 14 years old. This was due to the start of the Second World War, which meant that the school gradually closed down and the children were sent home. In some ways this was fortuitous, as she had not found school easy because of her dyslexia. Many years later describing her academic difficulties and gifts, she said:

'My school problems were appalling: spelling and hand writing, difficulty with maths formulas, and poor time keeping. I liked geometry and found my interests were three-dimensional. The dyslexic gift of being able to think in a holistic and three-dimensional way is something I shall always be grateful for'.

Above: One of the drawings in the portfolio that Susan presented for the Life Drawing Prize at the Royal College of Art in 1948.

This gift was eventually to lead Susan towards sculpture, but the first step was to study at art school. She went to Maidstone School of Art for one day a week for a term before gaining a place at Canterbury School of Art. Her journey to Canterbury was not easy, it involved cycling to Tenterden before catching the bus to travel the 26 miles to Canterbury. Her artistic talents were already quite well developed judging by the self-portrait on page 98, which she painted when she was 17 years old while studying at Canterbury. Susan found she was interested in so many things at art school, that when the time came to select an area in which to specialise, she found it terribly difficult to make a choice. Gradually she realised that she wanted to study sculpture and as Canterbury School of Art did not have a sculpture department she had to move. She chose to go to Guildford School of Art because of its good reputation in that field and started there in 1943. She studied painting and drawing with Raymond Coxon and pottery with Margaret Lockyer, the Principal. The Head of the Sculpture Department was Harry Parker, and after studying at Guildford for some time Susan told him, quite firmly, that she wanted to leave and go to the Royal College of Art in London. He was not keen on her leaving and said that in order to be admitted she would have to take the College entrance examination in sculpture at the same time as the Board of Education's drawing examination. He obviously felt that it would be a major hurdle to take the two examinations at the same time and thought that it was not possible to pass both in the same year. But Susan was not put off and so in 1945, much against the school's wishes, she took the examinations. She passed the drawing examination by just 3 marks. On hearing the news her father who had always been very encouraging, said: *'that was nicely judged!'*

Royal College of Art

While Susan studied at the Royal College of Art she shared a flat with an old school friend, Sylvia Priestley. Sylvia's father, J. B. Priestley, lived at The Albany, Piccadilly which was situated next to the Royal Academy. The Albany had been 'gentlemen's chambers' in the nineteenth century and Susan and Sylvia occupied the top floor, which had been the servants' quarters. J. B. Priestley's own flat, with its wonderful collection of paintings, was on the floor below. He was very interested in art and painted himself. The Albany was a very grand place and Susan can remember going back at the end of the day dressed in trousers smeared with clay to be greeted by the top hatted porters bowing and saying *'good evening'*. An hour later she would go out for the evening 'dressed to the nines' and the same porter with the same expression would bow in the same way. While she was there she went to the Chelsea Arts Ball with Guy Neale, who was a friend of hers from childhood when they had been next door neighbours. The Ball was preceded by a parade of floats and the Royal College had to design and dress a vehicle with a theme that was something to do with 'hell'. Susan went dressed as a dipsomaniac, but the evening almost turned into hell for her when the float ran over her foot. But she limped on to the ball and the couple of bottles of gin they smuggled in under their coats eased the pain!

During her time at the Royal College of Art, Susan found two people particularly helpful and influential. One was the sculptor, Frank Dobson, who was the Professor of Sculpture in Susan's second year. He introduced drawing classes for the students, which rather shocked them as they were not used to the idea that sculptors should be expected to draw. Up to this point they had been exempt from all the drawing classes because they were normally run at the Exhibition Road site. This was quite a way from the Sculpture Department which, at that time, was located in Nissan huts behind the Natural History Museum. Dobson hired a model and made the students attend evening classes in drawing in the sculpture building and, because they did not have to go to Exhibition Road, there was no excuse for not attending. Susan thought the drawing classes were marvellous and Dobson a superb teacher. *'He was not very good with words but he could illustrate his thoughts to us by waving his hands and drawing. He knew exactly what he was doing'*, she recalled.

Above: Two of Susan's drawings of birds that may have influenced her ceramic designs.

During Susan's third year at the Royal College of Art she won the Life Drawing Prize, which was open to all final year students at the College. Susan produced a portfolio of drawings, most of which she thought were awful, but to her astonishment Dobson said one was like a Leonardo da Vinci, which made her feel very proud. Susan also learnt her modelling techniques from Dobson and adopted the method he used of building up the surface by applying small pellets of clay. She liked to leave the rough surface on the finished work, as he did. This technique can clearly be seen in the head of her grand nephew, Thomas, photographed on page 100.

When Frank Dobson retired as Professor of Sculpture, John Skeaping moved from the Central School of Arts & Crafts to take the post. Apart from Skeaping's skills as a sculptor Susan also found him to be an excellent teacher who produced brilliant life drawings. Commenting on both Skeaping and Dobson Susan said: '*they both thoroughly understood the technique of drawing three-dimensionally, and could explain or demonstrate precisely what they were doing*'. Skeaping had won the Prix de Rome, the prestigious sculpture prize, jointly with Barbara Hepworth in 1925. Susan had enjoyed her time at the Royal College so much that when she got her ARCA in 1948 she did not leave but was awarded a 4th year, which she had been very keen to get. She was lucky, or more likely talented enough, to be given this extra year and had visions of taking the Prix de Rome herself, which would have allowed her to study in Italy for a year. However, in reality she rather wasted her 4th year because that was the year she married.

Left: Susan's first commission, an Ayrshire cow, modelled in 1947. 16 inches high and 20 inches long.

She first met her husband, Richard Parkinson who was two years her younger, in 1946 while she was in her second year at the Royal College of Art. Their mutual love of music brought them together. Susan had just been given her first commission, which was to design and make a model of a dairy cow. An agricultural council or dairy board of the time wanted a model of an Ayrshire cow in order to demonstrate its excellent milking qualities. As it was her first commission, Susan took the project extremely seriously and designed a model that could be separated into three wedge-shaped sections which helped to show the shape of a good milking cow. She was thrilled with the fee of £25 that the commission brought and she wanted to use the money to buy a gramophone, but unfortunately they cost more than £25 at the time. She explained this problem to Guy Neale, who was now in the Royal Air Force. On hearing her story he said that a friend of his made gramophones and that he could probably make one for her. The friend turned out to be Richard Parkinson and he did indeed build Susan a gramophone. The gramophone became Richard and Susan's most important possession and every time they moved house afterwards the gramophone was the first thing to be organised. This was not easy as, for example, the electricity in some of their houses was DC (direct current) and Richard had to make a transformer for the gramophone.

Before her 4th year at the Royal College Susan moved from The Albany to Holland House, a very elegant Georgian building that stood in the middle of a slum and bomb-site on the river Thames at Isleworth, London. One of its major attractions was its view of the river and the coal barges, which at that time regularly traversed the Thames. As the rent was so high she had to find someone else to share the house and so another girl from the sculpture school, Rita Ling, joined her. After a short while they found they were struggling financially and so they decided to let the third bedroom in order to improve their cash flow. After some discussion they decided to offer it to Richard, who was in the process of being de-mobbed from the Air Force. They were strongly influenced in their choice by the fact that he owned a car. He had a rather nice MG and this would give them access to transport, which was a distinct attraction as they were feeling rather isolated in Isleworth because it was a long way by bus from the centre of London.

A year later, in 1949, Susan and Richard married and so all Susan's grand plans for the Prix de Rome and Italy came to nothing. Richard got a job at the Foreign Office, which may have helped impress Susan's father but in reality it was a very menial job that involved fetching cups of tea and doing little else! They had little furniture in the house at Isleworth, but that did not matter, they had the gramophone and music. They painted a large chessboard on the floor in order to fill part of the empty space and make the lack of carpets and furniture less noticeable! The house also had three large dungeon-like basements and Richard transformed one of them into a sculpture studio for Susan. It was pitch dark as it had no natural light, but Richard, who was very clever with lighting, was able to turn the cellar into a useful space by setting up a variety of different lighting systems.

Early sculpture made at Isleworth

One of the first sculptures Susan made in the converted basement of Holland House was for Mr Prater. He was the curator of the Bird Department at the Natural History Museum immediately after the Second World War and had previously worked at the Bombay Natural History Museum. The Royal College of Art's Sculpture Department was situated just behind the Museum and Susan had often gone to the Bird Department to make studies. After the war the Natural History Museum was expanding and Mr Prater requested that Susan make a sculpture for the new area. She obviously had to create a sculpture of birds and she decided to make a model of terns. First she made the clay model and then a wooden version, but unfortunately the project came to nothing because funds for the building ran out. *'The first things to get cut were the artistic bits'* she commented. Another of Susan's very early sculptures was *the canteen woman*, made in reduced stoneware in either 1949 or early 1950. The *canteen woman* has the 'fashionable' hairstyle of the time, and was first exhibited in 1951 at *The Circle and The Square*, a London exhibition which was sponsored by the Council of Industrial Design.

Richard must have been impressed by his two flat mates and the teaching and approach of the Royal College of Art, as he decided that he also wanted to go to there. So, in 1949, he applied for and was awarded an ex-service grant to study pottery. Of course, without qualifications, he could not go to the Royal College directly and so he went to Guildford School Art where he took a joint art and pottery course and studied under Helen Pincombe.

Crowan Pottery

During the summer of 1950 Richard and Susan spent a very useful 10 weeks with Harry Davis at the Crowan Pottery in Cornwall. The Pottery had not been operating long as Harry and his wife had only purchased the land and buildings in 1946. In addition to the house and outbuildings the property also

Above: One of Susan's first sculptures, the "canteen woman", made from coiled clay in low-fired, reduced stoneware. 21 inches high. Original photograph by Henry Lewes.

included a mill with a water wheel, which during the war milled cattle fodder, but by 1950 Harry had turned the mill into a very efficient Pottery and ran all the machinery from the water wheel. He was an enormously skilled man and technically very proficient. *'The Pottery operated like a company production line at Stoke-on-Trent'*, Susan recalled. *'All the cups were precisely the same size and the glaze was always perfect'*. David Leach is quoted as describing Harry Davis as *'being as much an engineer as he was a potter'*. Because of his attitude Harry was a very good teacher and Richard learnt a considerable amount both about the technical side of potting and how a commercial pottery should be run. This knowledge was to prove invaluable later when the Parkinsons decided to set up their own Pottery.

While he was at Crowan Pottery Richard threw a certain amount of functional ware. This was useful as the technique was generally not taught thoroughly at Art Colleges. The pots and jugs Richard threw at Crowan were fluid in form; that is they had pronounced horizontal ribs left from the throwing process, and if the clay had to be pinched to form the lip of a jug it was done in a bold manner. These pieces have quite a different feel to the very precise and regular functional studio ware that Harry Davis was producing. Richard's pieces were marked with an impressed seal, with RP on it, on the side of the pot and an impressed mark, Richard Parkinson, on the base. Richard's Crowan pieces were decorated with free-flowing brush stokes known as 'squiggles', a form of decoration used on Crowan plates. Susan remembered that they called them *'May's squiggles'* because they were generally painted by May, Harry's wife. Susan already knew May's sister quite well because they had been to school together. May was a member of the Bruderhof, which was a very extreme religious sect. It was an international community rooted in Anabaptist and early Christian traditions, which was committed to non-violence, justice and fellowship. May had joined the sect during the Second World War and had gone to Paraguay with them. Back in England *'she went round Cornwall wearing black skirts that went down to the ground'*, Susan recalled. Harry and May lived a very strange life and had *'rows of children'*. In many ways Harry was years ahead of his time in that he did everything himself. He would not buy anything from anybody and was totally self-sufficient. This idea may have started with the concept of studio pottery, where traditional processes and materials were preferred to modern methods and technology by the majority of studio potters around the middle of the twentieth century. But Harry took this concept much further so that it pervaded all aspects of life; he even went as far as making his own bath!

Richard and Susan took advantage of their stay in Cornwall to travel round the county in their Land Rover and meet all the well-known potters working there. Richard was very interested in different clay-bodies and so the tour was particularly educational for him. The potters they visited included Bernard Leach and Michael Cardew. Michael Cardew lived in the middle of a marsh and they had great difficulty finding his Pottery, Susan recalled. Michael had a beautifully made, old-fashioned wheel that he turned by hand. He had designed the wheel himself and it was so well made that when he spun it once the momentum created was enough for him to completely throw a pot. Susan and Richard thought they ought to repay him for the time he had spent showing them around his pottery and talking to them about his methods and techniques. So even though they had very little money at the time they decided to purchase one of his pots. They pooled their money and managed to scrape up five shillings, which in those days was quite a considerable amount of money. This sum bought one of his mugs, which they kept and used for many years, but unfortunately today it is missing its handle and so Susan has planted a cactus in it!

Susan was supposed to be sculpting and doing woodcarving while Richard was learning pottery techniques from Harry Davis. This was not easy without the right materials. Richard would drag huge tree trunks from the marsh and expect Susan to carve them, but this was not possible because they were often rotten and far too damp to work with. Instead she spent her time doing the washing up in the stream and trying to find something to eat, which usually turned out to be toast and margarine. Harry's lifestyle was very

Above: Early functional ware thrown by Richard at Brabourne, Kent. His seal is visible under the handle at the base of the jug. The cup shows the two vertical lines which Susan commented on, see page 51. Photograph taken from a promotional leaflet for the Richard Parkinson Pottery.

Right: "Caged bird," 8 inches high, modelled in reduced stoneware and iron by Susan in 1951. Original photograph by Henry Lewes.

basic; what he was prepared to put up with himself was also thought to be good enough for everyone else. His idea of sanitation was described as *'simply appalling'*. There was no water closet; it all went on the carrot bed, and as a consequence he produced the most marvellous carrots. Because of the lack of this facility, Richard and Susan spent most of their meagre wage driving to Helston in order to visit the public lavatories. Harry was extremely mean with his rate of pay, probably because of his spartan outlook on life. He employed two students during 1950, including Richard, both of whom were paid £1 one week and £1.25 the following week. This was done in order to confuse the Inland Revenue, apparently.

The tiny caravan they lived in at Crowan was very damp, and it was a particularly wet Cornish summer. The caravan was heated by a calor gas stove that leaked and as a result Susan got some sort of poisoning and became quite ill. As they had given up their flat at Isleworth she went back to her family home in Tenterden to recuperate. Richard decided to leave Guildford School of Art, which was a long way from Tenterden, and look for a college nearby where he could continue his studies. He chose Woolwich School of Art, which had a very good reputation for sculpture. He started there in 1950 and studied under Heber Mathews from whom he learnt a lot and liked very much. Heber Mathews was quite old and rather deaf by the time Richard went to Woolwich but Richard, who was very good at getting information from people, did not find this a problem. Heber Mathews was very keen on bricks and he inspired this strange addiction in Richard too. Richard could identify any brick and he knew exactly what temperature a particular brick would stand, this knowledge was a great help when they set up their own pottery and had to build a kiln. Richard may well have inherited his technical and engineering skills from his grandfather, who had been an engineer in India. Although Richard had been brought up by his grandmother he did not know his grandfather who had died before he was born. But he had a number of fascinating technical drawings of bridges and other projects that his grandfather had designed and constructed in India.

Working as a sculptor in Tenterden
Susan had worked for a year teaching at Gravesend School of Art before they went to Cornwall but on her return, in the late summer of 1950, she did not get another job immediately. Instead she continued to work as a sculptor from her family home in Tenterden building up her models with coiled clay. Few examples of Susan's early work survive but a number of photographs taken by Henry Lewes admirably depict the dramatic nature of her sculpture. His photograph of the *caged bird*, which is an 8 inch sculpture in reduced stoneware with an iron cage, illustrates this well and provides an early indication of the form of her future porcelain designs. Susan went on to make a much larger version of the *caged bird* that was approximately 2½ feet high, but this was never exhibited because of its

Right: The head of "Diana" modelled by Susan in reduced stoneware. Original photograph by Henry Lewes, dated 1951.

Above: A double exposure photograph taken by Henry Lewes in 1951. It shows the original model of the unicorn, which is 18 inches high. The women behind the unicorn are musicians and were also modelled by Susan. They were almost 3 feet high and were made at Brabourne Lees, Kent in 1951 in the first kiln Richard built there. Susan made the musicians as large as the kiln would permit.

size. Many years later, in the early 1960s, she returned to this subject and designed a small porcelain model of a caged bird, see page 78. In the porcelain model the iron wire representing the cage is replaced by bent cane.

One of the difficulties with Susan's sculpture is in knowing how to describe it. It has a lovely colour which looks like faded terra cotta but in reality it is usually low-fired stoneware. The colour range created, which varies from pale to deep terra cotta, can be seen in the photograph of the mural on page 101 and the *female dachshund* on page 99. The stoneware model of the *female dachshund*, with its strong basic form and minimal surface decoration, except for the texture created by the pellets of clay, is typical of her early work. She developed the technique of exaggerating what she perceived to be the key features of the model. *Diana* is another stoneware model Susan made in 1950 or 1951; *'she is a very Betjeman-type of lady, not at all intelligent'*, Susan commented. The reverse of the original Henry Lewes' photograph has the inscription: *'Deep down the drive, grow the rhododendron. Deep down, sand deep..., etc.'* These models and other similar ones were exhibited in the early 1950s, and also at a major exhibition held at Primavera, London in 1955. All Susan's sculptures were exhibited and sold under her maiden name of Sanderson. Previous articles and books on pottery marks have suggested that she marked her early work with the stamp illustrated below. This is not correct. The image below was created Michael Goaman and Sylvia Goaman (neé Priestley) some time later for use on the Pottery's letterheads and cards. The only mark Susan used was her initials 'SP' which she first used on a business Christmas card she designed for Richard and herself in 1951. If appropriate she also used this mark on ceramics she had decorated such as the teapot photographed on page 105.

The move to Brabourne

At this point two things occurred which changed Richard and Susan's lives completely.   The first was that Susan's sister and brother in law had, very conveniently, bought Lodge House at Brabourne Lees, Kent during the summer of 1950. It was a large traditional, Kentish medieval house with an oast house, barn and stables. They lived in a flat above the oast house for the first few months while they refurbished the house. Once this was complete Susan's brother in law, Alick, with considerable generosity offered Richard and Susan the flat in the oast house and a stall in the barn to use as a sculpture studio. They gratefully accepted and moved there early in 1951. They were soon knocking down the partition between the first and second stalls in order to enlarge the workshop and not long afterwards they extended into the third stall as their creative work expanded. Richard built a kiln in the oast house to fire Susan's sculpture, and once Susan had a kiln that worked satisfactorily, so that she could fire her sculpture easily, a very productive period followed.

One of the first pieces Susan made at Brabourne Lees was the terra cotta mural of heads illustrated on page 101. The second was probably the large earthenware unicorn, illustrated opposite. This was the forerunner of the plaster of Paris models of the *lion and unicorn,* which were the second factor that changed their lives. Susan got the inspiration for the style she used for the models of the *lion and unicorn* from Arnold Machin's Zodiac Bull that was manufactured by Wedgwood & Sons.   The

Right: Henry Lewes' photograph of the plaster of Paris lion and unicorn decorated with ink that was published in the Architects' Journal of 9th October, 1952. The description beneath the photograph reads:
"The photograph .. shows examples of ceramic sculpture designed by Susan Sanderson in white glazed porcelain with lemon yellow, delft blue or lustre decorations. These designs, which are being submitted to the COID (The Council of Industrial Design) for approval as Coronation souvenirs, are produced by Richard Parkinson and Partners, a small country pottery in Kent built in an old stable and oast house."

Zodiac Bull was first exhibited at the *Britain Can Make It* exhibition, which was held at the Victoria and Albert Museum in 1946 and was the first event that the Council of Industrial Design organised. Susan was greatly impressed when she saw the bull and thought it would be good fun to try to produce a lion and unicorn in a similar style to coincide with the *Festival of Britain* in 1951. The Festival, which in terms of key concepts in art and design followed from the *Britain Can Make It* exhibition, was *'like a breath of fresh air'* and had a lasting affect on many designers and artists. Susan particularly liked the way that the exhibitors did not take themselves too seriously and perhaps she developed her tongue in cheek humour that comes across so well in her ceramic models as a result of this.

Susan made the models of the *lion and unicorn* but they were not in time for the Festival of Britain. She used waste moulding and piece moulding techniques for casting. These were the only methods used for sculpture and the only ones she had learned at the Royal College of Art. Because she was using this process she made the *lion and unicorn* models in clay and cast them in plaster of Paris, before painting them rather roughly with ink decoration. And so almost by accident she created the black and white style that was to become the signature of their pottery. During the first half of the 1950s Nicholas Vergette and James Tower were also using black and white decoration. Susan had always admired and loved their work, which can perhaps best be described as 'Festival of Britain style'. Anyone who started to design at that time would have absorbed this as part of the atmosphere of the period and Susan may have subconsciously imitated them although her rather humorous work could not be considered at all similar to the monumental style of James Tower, even though the styles of decoration have something in common.

Susan and Richard's friend Henry Lewes, who was a photographer and had studied at Guildford School of Art with Richard, took some photographs of the decorated plaster models. As he was doing free-lance work for the Architects' Journal he succeeded in publishing one of the photographs there together with the optimistic, accompanying description supplied by Richard. To everyone's absolute astonishment architects sent in orders for the two ink and plaster of Paris models! Perhaps this was because the timing of the publication of the photograph was fortuitous, as architects were beginning to become concerned with interior decoration as a way of showing off their buildings and were looking for objects that would help them achieve this. It was a period when the 'House and Garden approach' was very important and books such as *The Daily Mail Ideal Home Book*, which was issued each year, became very popular and tended to dictate taste. In addition the similarity the lion and unicorn bore to Arnold Machin's bull was very useful as the bull had been a great commercial success, and architects would have known this.

Initially the demand and interest of architects provided Richard and Susan with a sideline and a bit of fun. They decided that they could produce the ceramic models that were requested. Susan went back to see the mould-maker at the Royal College of Art to ask him to make the moulds for the *lion and unicorn* as neither she nor Richard had any knowledge of slip-cast mould making. *'He made the most beautiful moulds'*, Susan recalled, *'but moulds that were required for sculpture not the sort you would want for slip moulding in a Pottery where the casting process has to be quick'*. She also remembered that the mould-maker took a very long time to make the moulds and that she and Richard were very worried about this as they had a number of orders lined up which they had to fulfil. Once they had the moulds they set about creating a business. It was a brave step as they had little knowledge; in Susan's words they were *'absolute babes in the wood'* as far as pottery production went. But no project however large daunted Richard who always believed that not having done anything similar before was never an obstacle. To illustrate his attitude Susan commented that while they were in the West Country visiting Harry Davis they spent a considerable amount of time driving around Devon looking at a number of large, decaying mansions as Richard was keen to acquire one to renovate.

CHAPTER 2   THE POTTERY AT BRABOURNE LEES 1951 - 55

Above: The Pottery's first model, the small bird otherwise known as the Coptic bird, which is 3¾ inches high.

Below: Susan's drawing of the same model.

Starting the Pottery

When Richard and Susan first moved to Brabourne Lees Richard was still driving to Woolwich School of Art completing his studies. When he graduated in the summer of 1951 he was able to devote himself to the technical side of kiln building, etc. The first kiln he built at Brabourne was for Susan's sculpture and it allowed her to fire quite large models, up to 3 feet in size, to a relatively low temperature. She took advantage of the size and made the women with their musical instruments, photographed on the double exposure on page 16, as large as the kiln would allow.

At this stage Richard and Susan had some idea that they wanted to go in for pottery but they still had a lot to learn. During the early part of 1952 they were busy discovering how to slip cast, searching for a suitable clay body for slip casting, and rebuilding and improving the kiln so that it reached a satisfactory temperature for their chosen clay body. The latter was not easy and it took six years and a considerable amount of rebuilding before Richard had perfected the main pottery kiln. Despite doing all this preparation it was not until the publication of the photograph of the *lion and unicorn* in the Architects' Journal of October 1952 that they realised that running a Pottery was a serious business option. In order to create the business they needed funds to buy materials and equipment and so they formed a partnership: Richard Parkinson and Partners. Susan's friend Guy Neale became one of the partners and Henry Lewes who had inadvertently created the impetus for the Pottery was the first to invest in it, he put up £100 which was used to build their first pottery kiln that only reached a temperature of 850°C.

The first models

Although the reason for establishing the Pottery was the initial demand for models of the lion and unicorn they were not the first pieces to be produced. The first pottery model was not so ambitious, it was a little bird, 3¾ inches high, with a long beak. As a consequence collectors sometimes refer to it as a toucan but it was called the *small bird* at the Pottery and Richard always referred to it as the Egyptian Coptic bird. It is shown as model number 1 in the catalogues and the mould was the first that Susan designed and made herself. No doubt the shape of the bird was dictated to an extent by

Above: Susan's drawing of the model of the cow which was published in the 1955 catalogue.

Below: Susan's drawing of the model of the sheep published in the same catalogue.

the need to create a model that would be simple to cast but it also has great appeal and it set the standard for subsequent models. The inspiration for the design probably came from the stone sculpture of the *caged bird* that Susan had recently completed. As with all of Susan's designs she manages to transform her drawings into a three-dimensional form whilst still retaining the quality and detail of her drawn work through the intricacy of the decoration. The model of the *small bird* should not be confused with the much larger bird of the same shape, which was made slightly later.

The *lion and unicorn*, which were model numbers 2 and 3, provided the backbone of the Pottery's commercial success during its first few years. At approximately 7 inches high they are considerably smaller than Susan's original terra cotta model of the unicorn, which was 18 inches in height. The reduction in size was due to the impracticality of moulding, firing and selling large models. The ceramic models of the *lion and unicorn* missed the *Festival of Britain* by a year but appeared in plenty of time to commemorate the Coronation of Queen Elizabeth II. The models made for the Coronation have E ^{II} R painted on the front together with a motif, which is usually a fleur-de-lys, and the date, 1953, on the reverse side of the model, see page 101. Although they were always made and sold in pairs, the *lion* seems to be more common today, possibly because the *unicorn* occasionally developed a crack across the neck. This can be seen in the photograph at the beginning of Chapter 1 and is probably due to the neck, with the head turned forward, being the weak spot of the model. The description under the photograph that appeared in the Architects' Journal stated that they were *'available in lemon yellow, delft blue or lustre decorations'*. This was probably part of Richard's natural optimism as they did not produce lustre glazes for another ten years and it would have been particularly difficult and foolish to start a Pottery using lustre glazes. Whether yellow and blue glazes were initially used is uncertain because the *lion and unicorn* normally have a grey or grey-blue decoration, as do many of the Pottery's early models. They remained in production for many years and occasionally the year of production was included in the decoration.

The 4th and 5th ceramic models were probably the *cock* and *hen* as Susan remembers that they were very early models. However, in the 1961 catalogue they appear as model numbers 23 and 24 and so if they were originally models 4 and 5 the moulds must have been remade quite quickly for some reason now forgotten.

The *large cat*, model number 6 and illustrated on page 103, is one of the Pottery's tallest models at 14½ inches high. Susan developed this model from an idea she had had earlier when she made a much larger stoneware sculpture of a cat, known as the *tall cat.* The ceramic version of this model, known as the *large cat*, proved very successful for the Pottery and the first ceramic model Susan made was purchased by Geoffrey Dunn, the owner of Dunn's of Bromley, the department store. The pattern of creating a sculpture and then using the idea for a ceramic model was one that Susan employed a number of times. The large owl and the two 'St Trinians style' schoolgirls, discussed later in this chapter, are other examples of this. Occasionally the *large cat* was decorated in red iron and as a consequence appears mainly dark in colour, except for its eyes. But more usually the cat's body was covered with wax resist and so it appears mainly white with thin lines of sgraffito decoration in a grey or green-black colour where the wax had been scratched away.

The *money bear,* model number 7, followed the *large cat* and was the first money box the Parkinsons produced. It proved very popular, and was one of the models that continued in production at Cinque Ports Pottery, Rye, Sussex after Susan had closed the pottery at Brabourne Lees.

Left: The sheep which Susan based on a pregnant Greek sheep. Model number 8, height 6¾ inches, length 11 inches. In the collection of Elizabeth Lunato.

This style of black and white decoration, which is created using the wax resist technique, is very rare on the sheep as it was more time-consuming and hence more costly than painted decoration. The more usual decoration on the sheep is a series of wavy, coloured lines that resemble wool, see the drawing on the opposite page and the photograph on page 102.

Colour decoration

The *sheep,* model number 8, was the first to be decorated in colour. She is a rather fat Greek lady who is about to drop her lambs and is definitely not a goat though some have referred to her this way! The early models made from the *sheep* mould have squiggly lines of colour on the body which could vaguely be said to represent unravelled pieces of wool, as illustrated in Susan's drawing. This decoration is often painted in a yellow-brown colour, see page 102. Later black and white versions of the *sheep* may be painted in a similar style or they may have decoration similar to that in the photograph above.

The 10th model was probably the *cow*, which is very rare today as it was rather wasteful of kiln space and therefore cost more to produce. The *cow* is interesting because it is one of the very few Parkinson models to have been decorated with colour. Some models of the *cow* have large pink spots or solid circles painted on their flanks and others yellow splodges, which look rather like a three

Above: Susan's drawing for the first model of the large owl, model number 9.

Below: A ceramic model of the large owl which has a matt finish. 8½ inches high.

pronged amoeba, as in the drawing on page 20. Colour decoration was a problem as the choice of colours available to Susan was limited to a rather *'feeble pink'*, delft blue and a *'dirty yellow'* (not the lemon yellow that Richard had rather optimistically referred to). This was because they were the only underglaze colours that worked satisfactorily at the very high temperature that their porcelain body had to be fired to.

Apart from the *whale*, introduced in 1956 or 1957 and illustrated on page 112, the *sheep* and the *cow* are thought to be the only two models to be produced with colour decoration. The Parkinsons discontinued colour decoration after a short time, possibly because the colours they could achieve were not particularly attractive or striking. In any case fairly soon the black and white ware with its delicate lines created by the wax resist technique became their 'signature' and once they realised that this had happened they would not have wished to revert to colour.

Owl models

The *large owl* is model number 9. The idea for the ceramic model came from a sculpture of an owl Susan had made previously. The sculpture was exhibited later, in 1955, with other examples of her work at Primavera and she was pleased when someone who owned and collected owls bought the sculpture as she felt she must have captured the essence of the bird. The ceramic model of the *large owl* predates the similar but smaller version, *little owl*, which is model number 46. The model of the *little owl*, see page 24, fitted into the hand, or pocket, so well and comfortably that it became known as 'pocket owl' at the Pottery. The two owl models proved very popular and, along with the *mouse*, the *little owl* is one of the easiest models to find today. Because of their popularity the owl moulds were remade and updated in terms of style and shape in 1960. The later models are much squarer and flatter. One of the problems that can occur when making models with flat surfaces is a 'concave effect', meaning that the centre of the clay body can become depressed. In order to avoid this Susan probably erred on the safe side with the first owl moulds. But by 1960 when the later owl models were introduced she had gained confidence in the porcelain body, which by that time had been modified and developed considerably, and so she was able to make the later moulds very thin or flat.

Special orders

All of the Parkinson models were produced in two finishes, matt or glazed. How many of each finish were made depended on the specific customer order. Almost all of

Left: Adam and Eve, first made as a present for J. B. Priestley from his daughter Sylvia. 7½ inches high. This model is in the collection of Barbara McAdam-Seth.

Below: The cock and hen model numbers 23 and 24. This style of decoration, which is often in shades of grey, was used during the first few years of their production. The height of the cock is 12 inches.

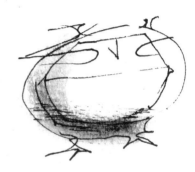

Above: Three drawings of owls by Susan, produced in 2004, and a little or 'pocket' owl, model number 46, height 3½ inches.

the Parkinsons' wares were made to fulfil a particular order but a few models were not. These models were known as 'kiln fillers' as they fitted well into the difficult corners of the kiln and so were fired rather than leaving the kiln space empty. The *large bird*, which was a larger version of the *small bird* and is illustrated on page 47, was a very useful 'kiln filler' and so it is another model that is quite easy to find today.

Occasionally the Pottery accepted special orders, which meant that Susan had to design a special mould. One of these orders was received in 1954 when Sylvia Priestley contacted Susan and asked her to make something special to celebrate her father's 60th birthday. As a result Susan made the model of *Adam and Eve*. Susan thought that the idea for the choice of *Adam and Eve* must have come from Sylvia and that the model was intended to be '*very primitive art, not very serious – just entertaining*'. Although it was a special order several models exist. It is normal with special orders to make several versions of the original in case the first does not fire well for some reason. But the model is also listed in the 1955 catalogue and so it was on offer to the world at large for a while and a few models at least must have been made. However, any further models would not have been decorated in the same style as the original one.

Susan received another special order through a personal connection. The request, from her cousin Paul Johnstone, was for two christening mugs for David Attenbrough's daughter Susan. Paul was a TV producer who trained David Attenbrough, and as he was very interested in marine archaeology the two men had quite a lot in common and became friends.

Richard and Susan were still experimenting whenever they had the time and this led them to try to make tiles by slip casting. The project was not a great success because slip casting was not a suitable method for tile production. However, a few tiles were produced and decorated and judging by the framed tile panel on page 110 they were very effective. The panel depicts one of Susan's favourite themes, musicians, and is of a slightly zany jazz group whose music is terrifying the cat which is about to take off in search of a noise-free place.

Models introduced in 1953/54

The model of the *large dog*, model number 19, is a French bulldog which Susan modelled on her own French bulldog bitch. She was black, hence her official name, *Ebony* but it was changed to *Ebony Beetle* and then to just *Beetle*. Everyone called her *Beetle* in the end and so this became the name of the porcelain model at the Pottery. The real *Beetle* was a great character apparently; she was very tough and had a strong sense of humour. She lived until she was 18 years old. The model of Beetle was first shown at an exhibition in Holland together with the *sheep*.

It was intended that the models of the *cock* and *hen,* model numbers 23 and 24, should be purchased as a pair. The Victoria and Albert Museum has an example of the *cock* and *hen* decorated in a brown pigment, which were bought from Primavera in 1954 for the equivalent of £3.25. The colour of the pigment changed over time according to the firing and recipe. The earlier pieces were either brown or grey rather than black but most people, including Susan, tend to prefer the greenish-black colour which they perfected a year or so later. The Pottery's 1955 catalogue states that the *cock* and *hen* were available unglazed in manganese (in which case the body appears dark brown with sgraffito lines revealing the white body beneath) or glazed in blue-grey. The cock and hen on page 23 are decorated in the 'glazed' style and the blue-grey is a similar colour to the decoration on the *sheep* illustrated on page 102. Note the easy and clever way Susan made the cock and hen stable, but yet made them appear realistic and light in form by painting the legs and feet on part of the base only. The *cock* and *hen* became important images for the business as they were used quite regularly on the cover of the Pottery's catalogues and advertising leaflets. The drawings on page 3 are Susan's and are the images used on the Pottery's promotional material. The *cock and hen* may have been chosen for this because they were the models purchased by the Victoria and Albert Museum and Richard and Susan would obviously have been pleased about the honour. Alternatively the drawings may have been selected because the models continued to sell well over the years and they are probably the most common of all the large models today. When Susan was shown round the Victoria and Albert Museum a few years ago she saw the models of the *cock* and *hen* with their brown pigment decoration. She told the curator, Oliver Watson, that she did not consider the brown glaze to be the best colour and, because of this, she would like to swap them for two models that were decorated in the more typical green-black colour. He said: *'absolutely, impossible! Once it is in the V & A you cannot take it out'*.

Above: Susan's French bulldog, Beetle. From a photograph in the collection of Ann Parr, neé Varrier.

Below: Susan's model of Beetle know as the large dog. Model number 19, height 8½ inches.

Left: Two cats, model number 33, 10 inches high. A model with a different style of decoration is illustrated on page 104.

Model number 33 is *two cats*; this is a model of two sitting cats joined at the body. These cats were also produced in two colour ways, either white with dark line decoration or dark greeny-black with sgraffito lines scratched through to the clay. These two colour schemes can be seen above and on page 104. Susan continually returned to cats as a theme and often depicted them in a similar stylised way. For example, there is a similarity between the heads of these cats and the head of the terra cotta sculpture of the walking cat illustrated on page 100. In their turn the *two cats* acted as a model for the *small cats* and the *cat pepper and salt,* which Susan designed some months later.

The two schoolgirls, models numbers 40 and 41, were another duo that were made and sold as a pair. They were known as *haystack hair* and *pigtails* at the Pottery because of their 'St Trinians' looks. As with the *large cat* the idea for the porcelain models came from original sculptures that Susan had made a few years earlier. The sculptures of the two schoolgirls were very important because it was while Susan was creating them that she realised she could make her models look larger than they really were by emphasising one dimension, the lateral in contrast to the depth. Because of this discovery quite a number of Parkinson ceramic models, starting with the *large owl* model number 9, are narrow when viewed from the side. The model of the *schoolboy,* which is a money box, was not made at the same time as *haystack hair* and *pigtails.* He is model number 107 and was probably introduced in 1958.

The Parkinsons also produced tableware that Richard threw by hand until 1955, by which time they had accumulated enough money to purchase a jigger and bat. The range of tableware gradually expanded and by 1955 the following items were listed in their promotional leaflet. Quite what was meant by 'celery bowls' is unclear. Susan remembers that they only made normally shaped circular bowls.

Breakfast cup and saucer
Porridge bowl
Small plate
Medium plate
Large plate
Lidded bowl and saucer
Mug
Small jug
Medium jug
Medium. large jug
Large jug
Small celery bowl
Medium celery bowl
Large celery bowl
Small flower pot and saucer
Medium flower pot and saucer
Large flower pot and saucer

The *three piping women*, see pages 30, 104 and back cover, were designed as a result of a weekend course Susan went on while she was still a student. The event was called the 'piping group' and was an occasion where people gathered to make and play musical instruments. The group consisted of just a few elderly gentlemen and a larger number of rather elderly ladies in hats that played their own handmade bamboo flutes with great enthusiasm. The average age of the members of the group was somewhere between 70 and 80, but the different characters amused Susan and she thought the weekend was a lovely occasion despite the fact that all the musicians were *'probably slightly bonkers'*! As a result she created the model of the *three piping women*. It was a simple two-piece mould, as the three ladies are joined together. The obverse is also rather good as they are sitting on chairs with elaborately painted backs. The average member of the public had obviously not come into contact with elderly, batty, musical ladies as the model did not sell well!

Above: The side view of haystack hair, model number 40, showing just how narrow the model is. This model is a late 1950s version with a matt finish and was exported to the USA. Height 7½ inches.

In order to make the moulds as simple as possible for casting purposes, Susan created several other models where the figures were joined in a similar way to the *three piping women*.   One of these is a row of birds sitting on the ridge of a house; it is photographed on page 103. It was known as *chorus of birds* at the Pottery and is model number 32. Another joined model is the *row of schoolgirls* which comprises five heads of 'St Trinians' style' schoolgirls and is model number 52, see pages 5 and 6. Yet another joined model portrays train commuters, and is entitled *The 8.15*.   Susan designed this model for the market in the USA and the inspiration came from her brother in law who used to travel to London every day on the 8.15 am train from Ashford.   He would do The Times crossword while watching his fellow commuters and Susan always found him very funny when he described the other people in the carriage.   She thought they all seemed to be very English and unsmiling, and tried to portray in clay the tight-lipped British character which she summed up as: *'we do not speak to our neighbours, we do not ask them the answer to 16 across'*.   Whether her brother in law, Alick, appreciated the model is a different matter!

Processes
The clay body
When Richard and Susan decided that they wanted to go in for slip-casting the first thing they had to do was to find a suitable clay body. Today a wide range of different clay bodies can easily be purchased from suppliers, but during the 1950s it was not possible to buy a ready-made porcelain or clay body anywhere. Nor could a new potter ask other, established potters for recipes as areas such

Right: A rather angelic-looking pigtails, model number 41, 7½ inches high. This model is as thin as haystack hair when viewed from the side. In the collection of Elizabeth Lunato.

Above: The 8.15, 6 inches high. In this model the left-hand commuter is reading the Herald, in another version he reads The Times.

as the potteries of Stoke-on-Trent guarded this type of knowledge jealously. It was considered to be a deadly secret; recipes for glazes and clay bodies would be passed down from father to son and only those who needed to know would be told. Often glazes would be mixed in a separate closed room away from the main pottery so that prying eyes could not see which ingredients were added in what quantities.

Consequently Susan and Richard had to experiment in order to find the best clay mix to use for their body. They bought truckloads of china clay from Cornwall and ball clay from Devon and set to work. They went through hundreds of trials in order to find something that was suitable for casting. In the end the most suitable body turned out to be a porcelain one. They had not intended to use porcelain; it just proved to be the first body that worked satisfactorily. *'In many ways it was an extremely stupid body to use'*, Susan recalled, *'as it was very expensive'*. Most of its expense lay in the fact that porcelain has to be fired to a higher temperature than other bodies and the Parkinsons had to use almost as much fuel to raise the temperature of the kiln the last 100°C to the required 1400°C as they had used to raise the temperature to 1300°C. It took Richard some considerable time to design a kiln to fire to 1400°C but eventually he succeeded. This was a mixed blessing as at that very high temperature *'things waved about in the kiln and were virtually liquid'*, as Susan put it. As a result there were a lot of seconds due to warping and cracking in the early days. Eventually they perfected their techniques and managed to fire at a slightly lower temperature.

Kilns
The initial problem was to get a kiln that would fire to such a high temperature as 1400°C. The first kiln Richard and Susan used was a coke-fired oven that they built themselves. It took 36 hours of one or other of them, or both, stoking away, for the kiln to reach 850°C; and what came out was still practically clay! Then, just before the Suez Crisis in 1956, they switched to an oil-fired kiln. This was not the best moment to do so because they found it very difficult to get hold of oil as a result of

the crisis, and the oil they did use was of poor quality and marked the glaze very badly. When oil was freely available again the kiln worked very well and was easy to control.

The oil-fired kiln needed electricity to operate, and so if there was a power failure the kiln cut out and the oil did not burn. This was definitely a fire hazard. In a way it was lucky that the bedroom was on the floor above adjacent to the kiln as Richard and Susan learnt the skill of listening in their sleep, so they would wake up if the kiln cut out. If it did, it meant that one of them had to get up in the middle of the night to see to it. On one occasion the kiln's supply of oil ran out at about 50°C short of the crucial temperature, this meant that the header tank had to be refilled by hand as quickly as possible. The header tank was situated directly above the kiln itself on a rickety, slatted and eminently burnable wooden floor on which the pots were put to dry. Richard had to climb up with a pan of oil and pour the contents into a small hole in the header tank without spilling a drop, as the kiln below was very hot and any spilt oil would have ignited immediately. Because the floor was so unreliable and rickety Susan held onto Richard's feet while he poured the oil. It must have been an awful moment!

Above: The three piping women, 11 inches long 8½ inches high. See also back cover and page 104 for reverse and different decoration.

Richard was always altering the design of the kilns but eventually, in 1957, he designed a large down-draught kiln with a muffle on one side whose chamber was about 4 x 3 x 3 feet. He got someone to come and help him build the kiln, as he was not very good at working on his own. It was his best design, especially the arrangement and design of the flues positioned at the bottom of the kiln. The flame went up and the flues then drew it back down so that the temperature was almost even throughout the kiln. David Leach visited them shortly after it was built and was so impressed with the design of the flues and the kiln that he borrowed the plans in order to build a similar one at his pottery. The year before, 1956, David had bought his own Pottery at Lowerdown Cross, near Bovey Tracey which he took over from Alfred and Lily Elhers.

Right: The oast house, which housed the kiln and the Parkinsons' living quarters, before the extension was built. From a photograph in the collection of Ann Parr, neé Varrier, she is standing in front of the oast house.

The colour variation between individual Parkinson pieces is usually due to their position in the kiln. On some pieces the dark, black colour has a very attractive green tinge to it, which some people prefer. This variation was caused by a temperature difference of around 10 or 15°C between the top and bottom of the kiln. Pieces placed at the bottom of the kiln tended to come out slightly darker in colour. The decoration on other pieces appears quite a pale grey or brown. These tend to be earlier pieces and the difference is caused, not by the kiln, but by the ingredients used.

Decorating

The normal colour was made from red iron, yellow iron and cobalt and it was usually applied before the biscuit, or first, firing, using the wax resist and sgraffito method rather than painting the colour directly on to the model. This method involved painting liquid wax on the model and then, with a fine metal tool, carefully scratching away the wax surface where the black colour was required. Finally the black colour was brushed all over the waxed model so that it sank into the white porcelain body through the crevices scratched in the wax. The wax barrier prevented the colour spreading across the surface and in the kiln, of course, the wax melted leaving the white porcelain beneath. For Susan's style of decoration sgraffito was a much better technique than painting the colour on by brush as the detail could be much finer and more precise. Richard and Susan developed the use of the wax resist technique in this particular way themselves. But to achieve certain effects on some models, or some areas of models, the colour was directly painted on with the brush. An example of this is the eyes and the hair of the *male* and *female classical heads*, model number 42 and 43, photographed on the next page. The model of the *schoolboy* is another example of this, his cap and the stripes on his jacket are painted by brush and the details of his face and school badge are created by applying the colour through wax, see page 64.

31

Left: The two classical heads, model numbers, 42 and 43. 7½ inches high. The eyes and hair are created by painting and the colour on the clothes and base by wax resist and sgraffito. This female model was made for the home market rather than the USA because her nipples are painted in!

Once the painting was complete the ceramic was fired in the gloss kiln. If the required finish was matt, this was the only firing needed, but if a glossy finish was requested the model would be dipped in glaze and fired a second time. Whilst only firing matt models once clearly had financial advantages as well as making the application of wax slightly easier, it had one major drawback. This was that anyone handling the models between decorating and firing had to be very careful where they placed their fingers because if they touched the painted surface the colour would smudge or come off. It was particularly difficult to stack the kiln tightly without touching any decorated surface.

Sales outlets

The Pottery's first retail outlet was the London gallery, Primavera, whose proprietor was Henry Rothschild. *'He was very supportive to us'*, Susan recalled, *'it was entirely due to him that the cock and hen went to the Victoria and Albert Museum. He was an enormous encouragement to a lot of young designers'*. His taste and ability to pick winning talent was obviously excellent as he was one of the first people to exhibit work by Lucy Rie.

When Richard and Susan were looking to add new outlets they soon realised that it was no good going to the head of the china department in large stores. This was because the china department was usually run by a tough middle-aged lady, *'who was only interested in grinding you into the floor saying firmly "that no this will not sell"'*. Eventually Richard and Susan determined that the best approach was to talk to the managing director, assuming, of course, that it was possible to make personal contact with him. One of the first people they approached in this way was the Managing Director of Heal's. They also went to Dunn's of Bromley and made an appointment to see Geoffrey Dunn who was enchanted with their models. They usually found that the top people in the firm liked their ceramics

Opposite: A photograph from House and Garden, December 1953 showing three Parkinson models as suggested Christmas presents. They are at the bottom left and are the cow, sheep and money bear.

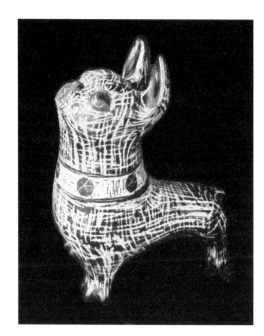

Far left: Susan's drawing for the model of Beetle.

Left: An early version of the model of Beetle, 8½ inches high, showing an unusual style of wax resist and sgraffito decoration which took far too long to decorate - hence its rarity! Detail from the 1955 catalogue.

Note the similarity in style of Beetle's collar between the drawing and the model. Later the collar became wider and the motifs less important, as in the photograph on page 25.

and understood the whimsical humour, but the tough, hard-nosed heads of the stores' china departments obviously did not.

By the end of 1953 Richard and Susan had been successful in establishing a core of good quality outlets and as a consequence their pottery was featured in a photograph in the magazine *House and Garden*, December 1953 which was part of an article suggesting stylish presents for Christmas. The photograph shows three of the Parkinsons' models: the *cow*, *sheep* and *money bear* that could be purchased from stores such as Dunns of Bromley for 50/-, 83/6d and 17/- respectively. (That is £2.50, £4.18 and £0.85.) Looking at the prices today perhaps the surprising fact is that the sheep sold for so much more than the cow as they are virtually the same size.

Eventually, by 1955, Richard and Susan succeeded in getting themselves acknowledged as 'a worthwhile call' by buyers who came from the USA. This meant that instead of Richard or Susan having to go to London, where they had to queue and wait interminably to see them, the buyers now came down to visit them at the Pottery. Susan remembered one occasion when a London taxi turned up with an American buyer. (Brabourne Lees is about 50 miles from London.) The taxi-driver parked the taxi, with its clock ticking away, outside the Pottery and waited for the buyer to return, which he did an hour and a half later. Susan was so agitated about the American's taxi bill that she did rather a poor job selling the wares and as a consequence the Pottery did not do as well as it should have in terms of orders that day.

Students

The Parkinsons took on students particularly during the first few years they ran the Pottery. The idea was that the student would learn the techniques and practices of a working pottery while helping Richard and Susan with production. It was in effect a type of short, informal apprenticeship. George Keck was their first student; he worked at the Pottery for about six months and was one of Richard and Henry Lewes' friends from Guildford School of Art. He was followed by David Mc Dowell and then David Bragg, who was the son of Sir Laurence Bragg the Nobel Prize winning physicist and head of the Cavendish Laboratory, Cambridge.

Every student had the job of keeping Susan's much-prized gramophone fed with records. Richard had a marvellous collection of 78 rpm jazz records which included Jelly Roll Morton and Bix Biderbecker. Music would be playing the whole time, Susan remembered. They needed something stimulating to keep them awake apparently, this was probably true in the evening when they were stacking the kiln, and so the job of the visitor was to make sure that the gramophone was never silent.

Henry Rothchild introduced one of Susan and Richard's student-workers; he was Herman Zaalberg, who came from a family of Dutch potters. Herman's grandfather set up the pottery, Zaalberg Keramiek, in the 1920s and by the 1950s it was being run very successfully by Herman's father, Meindert. Henry Rothchild visited their Pottery in the Netherlands while on a purchasing trip for his gallery and they discussed the possibility of getting an apprenticeship and labour permit for Herman to visit the UK. This Rothchild duly did and Herman went to the Rye Pottery in Sussex for six months. While he was there he introduced them to new methods of work which included 'dry throwing'. Dennis Townsend, who was one of Rye Pottery's apprentices at the time, said: *'it was an education to watch him throw this way, no slip no mess'*. Herman was not very keen on the clay body Rye Pottery used, and as one of his reasons for coming to England was to learn more about porcelain techniques he was keen to move on. So six months after he had joined Rye Pottery he was looking around for another placement when he met Henry Rothchild again in Primavera. Herman liked Hans Coper's work, which was similar to his father's, and he was also very keen on the work of Lucy Rie and he wanted to learn her techniques. Unfortunately she could not take him at the time and so, influenced by Henry Rothchild, his second choice was Susan and Richard.

Having obtained his work permit Herman started working at the Richard Parkinson Pottery in March 1954. He spent the first month sleeping in the rather damp summerhouse at Lodge House before finding a room in Sellindge. He had become used to regular working hours at both Zaalberg and Rye Potteries but the Parkinsons did not work that way and so sometimes when he arrived for work in the morning he had to wake them up! At the other end of the day they continued working while he went

Above: Haystack hair and pigtails, model numbers 40 and 41, 7½ inches high. These versions do not look to be the most trustworthy of characters in the school!

Right: A small dish, 3¾ inches in length, designed and decorated by Guy Neale in 1954. Note his initials on the hat. Most of Guy's work appears to have been marked in a similar fashion.

back to his digs because if he stayed too late in the evening his landlady became rather angry. Whilst Herman learnt a certain amount about the techniques of slip casting, etc. he commented that *'he learned more about a style of life than porcelain'*. When he first arrived at the Pottery he thought one had to work all day as had been the case at Zaalberg and Rye Potteries, but by the time he left he had seen that Scarlatti, jazz and sunshine belong to life as well and that they could be absorbed into one's work and make an important contribution to it.

It was quite a fortuitous introduction and arrangement for Susan and Richard as Herman later suggested they exhibit at a gallery in the Netherlands. The exhibition took place in 1955 and Susan's model of her dog, *Beetle*, was first exhibited there. This in turn led to several Dutch department stores, including the Amsterdam companies of Focke en Meltzer and DeBijenkorf, stocking their ware. In both cases Herman visited the stores to show them the Parkinsons' work.

In 1957 Heidi, a German student who was a friend of Herman's, came to England to work at the Pottery. One of her favourite techniques was to roll the clay into very thin strips and make small models which looked like fine wrought iron. She made models of the *lion* and *unicorn* this way, but not many of these were made and sold because they were very fragile, and so they are very rare today. Heidi was followed by another German student, a mould-maker, and because one pottery rarely has enough work for a full-time mould-maker the Parkinsons shared her with Rye Pottery.

In addition to the students, Guy Neale, who had been a friend of Susan's for many years and was also a partner in the business, came to work at the Pottery in 1954. He was also mad about jazz and so he fitted in well and remained for a couple of years, becoming a director when the Pottery changed from a partnership to a limited company, before leaving to work in Spain. Guy was principally a surrealist painter, one of his paintings is illustrated on page 112, but for several years prior to working at the Pottery he had been working on animation for a film company in Waldorf Street, London. Previously he had refused to do official training at any College of Art instead he went to France and largely taught himself. The Parkinsons gave him a room to use as a painting studio while he was at the Pottery and he also did a certain amount of work in ceramics, but he was rather disappointed with the lack of colour in the Pottery's range. In order to overcome this he tried to use red iron to produce more colour but this produced a pale mid-brown colour and so was not considered very successful, but it is a very pleasant subtle colour. He also used a deep blue, slightly grey glaze on a few items, and he or Susan also did tests with a midnight blue glaze but this does not seem to have been used on production pieces. He generally painted his ceramic work rather than using the wax resist and sgraffito technique and so his work can quite easily be identified because his decoration is slightly different in style and not so delicate as the Pottery's normal ware. The little dish with its General-like figure with Guy's initials on the hat illustrates his style very well. Guy also designed the Pottery's first bottle stoppers which were military and appear to be heads of a cavalry officer, grenadier guard and French gendarme. These moulds were re-made later when the Pottery introduced them into their normal production range.

Time off
Richard was keen on fast cars and flying. Much of his spare time was taken up renovating classic cars. Herman Zaalberg remembered a trip to Farnborough Air Show where the first Delta aeroplane was shown and the sound barrier was broken. They drove at break-neck speed to the aerodrome and had a wonderful picnic on the grass while surveying the landscape. Richard took up gliding with his usual *'I am going to get to the top'* attitude. He became a member of the Kent Gliding Club and eventually became their Chairman. He was very keen on gliding and while most beginners look forward to the moment when they go solo for the first time Richard determined from the beginning that he would fly for England. This attitude must have been exceedingly tiring to live with because it usually meant that everyone around him had to help translate his visions into reality. Susan recalled that he always expected her to cook a beautiful meal while either decorating the last piece of pottery for the kiln or holding things to be put in the kiln. Later, when they had employees, Richard and Susan would occasionally leave them to finish off for the day and pack the kiln if the wind was suitable for gliding.

Above: One of the Pottery's standard triangular-shaped dishes, decorated rather unusually with the head of a girl similar in style to the model haystack hair. 6¼ inches across.

CHAPTER 3   EXPANSION AT THE POTTERY 1955 - 58

Right: The Pottery after it was enlarged. The new extension is centre right, with the original oast house behind. The corner of Lodge House is on the left hand side of the picture. From a photograph in the collection of Ann Parr, neé Varrier.

Expansion

As the business grew Richard and Susan naturally concentrated on different aspects of running the Pottery because of their very different talents. Richard was in charge of the technical side of the business and also the marketing, which largely meant driving round obtaining orders. It was a job he was well suited to because of his love of cars and driving and also because he had plenty of confidence and was not afraid to take on the most unapproachable of ceramic buyers. This left Susan free to concentrate on designing but, of course, she also made the moulds, decorated the ceramics and packed them for despatch. Towards the end of 1954 the business was growing at a considerable rate and it became clear that they could no longer manage in the existing space and without assistance. The oast house had a barn attached to its east side and they wanted to refurbish this area in order to create a number of different workrooms. This was going to cost around £2,000, which was a considerable amount of money in those days. In order to raise the finance for the alterations Richard and Susan decided that they should turn the business into a limited company.

The next step was to draw up plans and apply for planning permission. Before giving planning permission the Local Authority insisted that the plans were altered to include a very expensive fire door on the ground floor between the new and old buildings. The old building, the oast house, housed the kiln and the purpose of the fire door was to prevent a kiln fire spreading through the building. Susan made the point that this was to protect the new building itself rather than the people working and living there. Their living quarters were still upstairs in the old building and their bedroom was almost directly above the kiln. There was no vertical barrier to stop a fire and obviously the planning department did not care whether they got burnt as they slept! The required fire door was obviously a sore point and was clearly remembered by Ann Varrier, their first employee, as being massive and ugly.

They needed to take on staff as soon as there was adequate space in which they could work. Their first employee was Ann Varrier, who had been sent to the Pottery for a job interview by the Ashford Careers Office at the beginning of 1956. She was employed to help Susan with the decorating, but to start with she had to learn to handle the wet pots and to fettle and sponge the models. She also learnt to pack the kiln and pack the ceramics for despatch. Soon after she started work Norman Bailey was employed to pug the clay and make the slip. Initially, when they were not busy with production work, the two employees were roped in to help paint the walls and doors of the new building. The extension, completed early in 1956, increased the working space considerably. It included a separate mould-making room, decorating room, storeroom and packing room as well as a small upstairs office above the storeroom. There was also a 'back room', which sometimes had seconds for sale and the Pottery had regular customers for these items. The meter reader was one of the customers. He used to buy one or two small items each quarter when he came to read the meter, so that in the end he had quite a large collection. Another collector was a local artist who purchased larger items such as the *barrister*, *cavalier*, *large cricketer* and the *lion and unicorn*.

Staff

Orders for the pottery continued to roll in, largely due to an increase in business from the USA. In order to meet the increasing demand more staff were taken on. Robert Hover and Jean Rogers were the Pottery's next employees; they joined in the summer of 1956. Susan taught Robert how to make the plaster moulds and Jean, who was 15 years old, took over much of Ann's previous role, leaving Ann free to concentrate on decorating. In time Jean became quite an expert at applying the glaze. She also packed the kiln, packed the pottery for despatch and in between drilled holes in the salt and pepper pots. The salt and pepper pots were a recent addition to the product range and proved very popular. Norman Bailey left the Pottery early in 1957 not long after Robert and Jean were employed and was replaced by Colin Newman. These four employees became the core workers and Susan and Richard came to rely on them.

Above: Margaret Chapman fettling. A decorated model of the barrister is on the top right shelf. Undecorated models include: pigtails, cat pepper and salt (far left), vinegar bottle, money bear and robin (bottom left). From a photograph by Henry Lewes, now in Margaret's collection.

Virtually all the employees came straight from school at the age of fifteen and were trained at the Pottery. They did not take any art school courses. Once the Pottery grew there were usually three girls fettling and decorating, a mould maker and one boy who was permanently employed casting and making-up the clay. The latter was quite a time consuming job as the clay had to be made from scratch in those days and had to go through the blunger and through the filter press before being dried. Margaret Chapman was the third decorator to be employed and Jean Dalrymple and Roy Hodges were two of the workers who joined the Pottery later on. The staff started work at 8 am and worked until 6 pm with 1½ hours off for lunch. The long lunch break was to allow the employees time to go home for lunch, as the Pottery was situated in a country village this usually meant quite a long cycle ride to and from home. They also worked on Saturday morning until 12.30 or 1 pm. The rate of pay was around £2.75 per week, depending on experience. They also had the added benefit of tea, morning and afternoon, which was brought down by Mrs Hodges, the 'daily' from Lodge House in a silver teapot together with Bath Oliver biscuits. On a more prosaic note, they also had their overalls supplied and laundered free of charge.

David McDowell, a friend of Richard and one of the Pottery's ex-students, came down from London to help out on one occasion. He supervised the Pottery while Richard and Susan took a long weekend off to go gliding in the Peak District. Ann recalled: *'It was to our credit being a young workforce that we all worked as hard as normal during this time, but we did have a bit of fun at lunchtimes. He had us girls shrieking with laughter, and taking his denim jeans in at the seams, to make them 'drainpipe' so that he could go jiving in London, which was beyond our imaginations at the time'.* Richard did not think in quite the same way about their high jinks when he returned home and so David was not asked again.

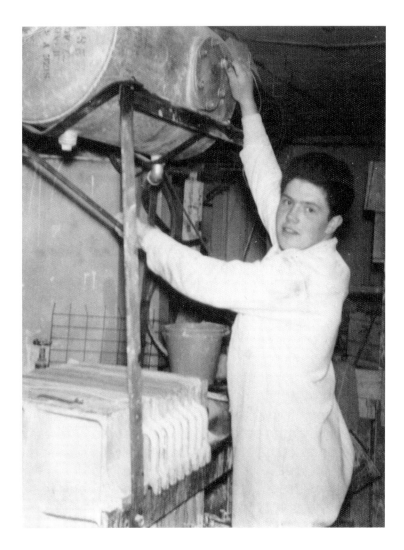

Right: Colin Newman operating the tank which held the slip used for casting. From a photograph by Henry Lewes, now in Colin's collection.

Above: Ann Varrier, left, and Jean Rogers fettling models. Jean is standing behind the noisy dust extractor, which the Pottery was obliged to install in order to comply with the Factory Acts. Two large mermaids can be seen on the middle shelf behind Ann. From a photograph by Henry Lewes in the collection of Ann Parr, neé Varrier.

Processes
Making the clay
The raw materials for the clay arrived at the Pottery in powder form and were turned into plastic clay as required. Four ingredients were mixed in varying proportions to form a suitable body; they were, ball clay, china clay, felspar and quartz. From time to time Susan and Richard would change the proportions of the constituents or try new additives, sometimes this would be successful but on other occasions the model might warp or even explode in the kiln. In order to monitor the progress and success of the new clay, a small mark, such as a cross or the letter O or Y, was stamped on the base. These small marks can be seen on the base of many of the smaller porcelain items, which suggests that they were frequently experimenting and testing new mixes and methods.

The clay mixture was put through the blunger which mixed the different constituents and particles in water and then, in order to remove the water, it was put through a press. The press contained a cloth that acted as a sieve and so the water was squeezed from the clay. The resulting clay came out of the press in cakes, which were then left to dry above the kiln. If the clay were to be used to make plates it would be put through a pug mill to remove any air. The remaining clay was turned into liquid slip which was used for pouring into the moulds, this was stored in the large tank pictured on the previous page.

Above: Ann Varrier applying liquid wax, the smoke from the paraffin lamp warming the wax is clearly visible. One of the theatrical figures is by her hand. Note the generous-sized chequer pattern cup and the typical Parkinson shaped dishes on the shelves. From a photograph by Henry Lewes in the collection of Ann Parr, neé Varrier.

Decorating

There were normally three girls engaged in decorating and related work at the Pottery at any one time. One would be a skilled decorator and the other two would be in the process of being trained. Susan usually worked in the decorating room with the girls, but occasionally she could be found in the mould-making room. When they first started work at the Pottery the trainee decorators had to do the fettling before graduating to the more skilful job of decorating itself. Fettling involves scrapping the excess clay from the porcelain model so that the joins in the mould cannot be seen. Moulds are made in a number of different sections, which are taken apart once the clay has dried so that the porcelain model can easily be extracted. The liquid clay tends to seep slightly through the joints in the mould forming ridges or raised lines on the clay model. These have to be removed, that is trimmed or fettled, before the piece is ready for decoration, so that the lines of the finished product are smooth. Fettling is rather a dusty job because the clay crumbles as it is scrapped away.

One day several *Factory Act* officials visited the Pottery and declared it to be 'a factory' and said that as a consequence the Parkinsons must have a dust extractor in order to remove the clay particles from the air. This large piece of equipment can be seen in the photograph on page 42. Jean would stand on a box to fettle so that she could see over the extractor and talk to Ann, not that much talking was possible because the machine was very noisy. Jean's box became a standing joke and every time Richard and Susan left the room the machine would be turned off, so the whole thing was rather pointless.

Once the ceramic had been fettled, the decorators brushed on the liquid wax that was to form the resist or barrier. This might be thought to be a simple task but it required a certain level of skill because the wax had to be the right consistency and this took some time to learn and get right. The Pottery used ordinary candle-wax, which had to be 'watered down' in order to make it thin enough so that it flowed over the surface of the clay. It was much easier for the decorators to apply the wax if the clay was only 'leather dry', that is firm to the touch but not fully dry. But usually by the time the decorators got round to decorating the ceramic models they had dried completely and the job became more difficult. The model was put on a turntable and then, using a brush, it was normally completely covered in wax. When the wax had been applied satisfactorily, the decorator would cut through the surface by scratching carefully with a thin tool.

A few models were waxed up to the head only, and on some the reverse applied and only the head was waxed. In this case a section would be cut out for the eyes and any other areas that were to appear black on the completed model. Sometimes the work would be divided so that Susan would cut or scratch through the wax and someone else would apply the colour or, alternatively, Susan would paint the eyes and another person would finish the decoration. One of the decorators, Ann, became extremely proficient and she was capable of decorating the theatrical figures, which are discussed in detail in Chapter 5. The theatrical figures had some of the most delicate and detailed decoration and, in addition, because of their shape they were very difficult to pick up and move during production without marking the surface.

Making the moulds

Initially, because of her training as a sculptor, Susan made the original models for the moulds in terra cotta. This meant that a mould had to be taken from the clay model, and this was then used to make the master mould. Once the master mould was created, the mould that was to take the liquid porcelain was made from the master. This mould would have a limited life and when it became worn a new, identical one could be made from the master, hence the name. But this method of creating a mould was unnecessarily lengthy. Quite soon Susan changed the method of modelling and thereafter usually made the original model from either araldite or fibreglass. Because the fibreglass, or araldite model was so much harder it could act as the master model itself, thereby cutting out a stage in the manufacturing process. Araldite and fibreglass could also be carved and so they had the advantage of giving a sharper outline to the finished product. Susan had to completely alter her modelling technique in order to use the new materials, as she had to carve material away rather than build up the model with small pellets of clay. When the mould was made from the model it was given a sequential number and this was also the number given to the model in the Pottery's catalogue. No more than 500 models would have been made from any mould, except possibly the very small ones such as the mouse, and some moulds were only used a few times if customers did not order that particular model very often. The moulds that were in frequent use would be placed on top of the kilns so that they dried quickly and thoroughly and could be reused without too much delay.

Once the Pottery expanded and employed staff, Susan had little to do with the moulding process. She still designed many of the moulds herself but she had taught Robert Hover, the mould maker, and he ran the moulding room on a day-to-day basis. Robert proved to be a very good mould-maker and by 1959, when the Pottery made the theatrical figures that were cast from very complicated moulds, he had the skill to deal with them. This was important because when Susan created the original models for this series she wanted to be able to concentrate on getting the likeness and character of the person rather than having to consider the construction of the mould itself. Up to that point she had always had to create models which could be made from relatively simple moulds comprising only

Right: Jean stacking the kiln for a gloss firing. The top row consists mainly of female classical heads but on the left there are two models of the woman knitting, one facing the door with only her left-hand side showing and on her left is another with her back to the kiln door. Underneath there are money bears covered in white glaze and beneath them stripey money cats. From a photograph in Jean's collection.

Above: Ann decorating a policeman, model number 85, circa 1958. Paint has previously been applied with broad vertical brush strokes and she is now doing the sgraffito work on his jacket. Two models of the bull are in the foreground and the right side of a model of Beetle is just visible. From a photograph by Henry Lewes in the collection of Ann Parr, neé Varrier.

Right: The large bird often used as a kiln filler. 6½ inches high.

a few pieces. However, by the time she made the theatrical figures she was able to design models that required moulds of 6, 7 or 8 pieces because she knew Robert had the skill to create them. It was a great tragedy, therefore, when Robert was killed in 1961. He celebrated his 20th birthday at a local pub and was riding his bike home that night when he had a minor accident that had devastating consequences. He was the one person at the Pottery that the Parkinsons did not have an understudy for. They expected the young girls to leave to get married or have children but they assumed that Robert would be there for many years, or if he did decide to leave they presumed that there would be time for him to help train someone else before he went. Because there was no understudy Susan had to take over all the moulding work again on Robert's death.

Packing the kilns

With the increase in sales in the mid 1950s the kiln had to be fired more or less non-stop. As soon as it was cool enough to unpack, it would be unpacked and reloaded, this meant that it was fired at least twice a week, once for biscuit and once for glazed ware. As the business continued to grow two kilns were needed and so Richard built a smaller kiln. It was intended that the small kiln should be used for lustre and glazed ware but it was not until the 1960s that Susan started to produce lustre ware and so the second kiln was normally used to relieve the pressure on the larger kiln and to process small orders that were required urgently. So in reality the two kilns were fired more or less alternately and both were used for biscuit (matt) and glazed ware as required.

When the working day finished and the staff had gone home Susan and Richard would start to pack the kiln, a job that took them at least two hours to complete. This was because every model could only go in certain places in the kiln due to its particular temperature and airflow requirements. In addition every square inch of the kiln needed to be filled and used because of the great cost of firing to such a high temperature. Susan remembered that she spent hours standing in the entrance to the oast house holding up the heavy boards with the biscuit models on them. The entrance was like a funnel focusing the draught that seemed to come from the Antarctic, and as it was the end of the day she would be feeling tired, cold and hungry as she stood there. Sometimes it would be 10 o'clock and totally dark before they would get a chance to warm themselves and get something to eat. *'Potting is a very tough 24-hour a day job'*, Susan recalled and this task obviously left a lasting memory. After loading the kiln, she would usually stay up until 4 am kiln watching, at which hour Richard would take over the watch. Susan found that the time she spent watching the kiln was the only time she had that was free and without interruption and so she used it for designing. As a consequence, to this day she still does much of her creative work in the early hours of the morning.

Later on Jean Rogers often packed the kilns in the evening for Susan, this meant that Jean stayed as late as 1 o'clock in the morning on rare occasions. She quite enjoyed the job because the Parkinsons often brought her a mug of beer while she was working, which was quite a treat for a 16 or 17 year old. They also gave her a lift home, of course, and said that she could start half an hour later the next morning so that she could catch the bus rather than cycle to work. This was necessary because her bicycle would have been left at the Pottery. Jean remembered that when she packed the small kiln she had to use a Tilly lamp for light because the kiln was situated in such a poorly lit area. Good light was vital in order to make sure that the pieces were as close as they could be to one another in the kiln without actually touching each other. Jean tended to carry the lamp around the Pottery with her and she also used it when decorating.

Backstamp
Susan did not often mark her own ceramic work but if she did she would use the initials SP, this can be seen in the close up photograph of the cat painted under the handle of *Nellie teapot* illustrated on page 105. Richard used a seal, which had 'RP' and 'B' for Brabourne on it, on his hand-thrown ware, see Appendix 2 page 97. Guy Neale usually signed his ceramic work within the design with his initials in lower case; this can be seen on the hat on the dish photographed on page 36.

The early models made at the Pottery were not often marked, but those that were had an impressed linear mark 'RICHARD PARKINSON' on the base. Towards the end of 1954, when the Pottery became a limited company, a metal stamp with 'Richard Parkinson Ltd' was introduced which created an indented mark in the base of models. The mark is oblong in shape but is very small and as a consequence is difficult to read. All export items had to be marked 'Made in England' and so all ceramics going abroad had to have either a separate 'Made in England' stamp or have the words incorporated into the normal mark. A separate mark was created and used as an additional stamp when the Pottery first started exporting. Later the words were incorporated into the main Pottery stamp. If a piece is marked 'Made in England' it was *probably* intended for the USA market, which was

Left: The small pepper and salt, 3¾ inches high, model number 60. In the collection of Elizabeth Lunato. This was one of the moulds which was later used by the Cinque Ports Pottery, Rye.

Left: Cat pepper and salt pots, model numbers 64 and 65. The salt, on the left, is 6 inches high.

by far their largest export market. But whoever applied the mark may have erred on the safe side and stamped all pieces in the batch with the 'Made in England' mark regardless of their destination.

Eventually an almost circular, impressed mark became the official stamp. This has 'Richard Parkinson' round the outside and 'Porcelain Made in England' in the centre, see Appendix 2 page 97. Sometimes an impressed mark that is just a 'P' was used. This was designed for use on very small pieces that could not take the full mark, but sometimes, if it came to hand, it was used on larger pieces as well. All the marks are very small and impressed except for one larger, black-ink mark which has 'RICHARD PARKINSON' arranged in circular form around 'PORCELAIN' on one line and 'MADE IN ENGLAND' on the next two. This mark is probably a later mark and was used on items exported to the USA.

For some reason the Pottery went through various stages when either the decorators or slip-casters put the backstamp on the models. Some models also have a small impressed symbol, these include a cross within a diamond, a small circle and a letter Y; as stated earlier, their purpose was to identify the success or otherwise of new clay bodies.

Advertising
A catalogue/leaflet advertising the Pottery's wares produced in 1955 describes the business this way: *'Richard Parkinson Ltd is a small group producing fine Porcelain and Terra cotta jugs, bowls, flowerpots and saucers which are hand thrown by Richard Parkinson and decorated in underglaze colours. Susan Parkinson, a sculptor, designs Ceramic figures and executes individual pieces in*

Left: Large pepper, vinegar and salt pots showing the three main styles of decoration used on them. The pepper on the left is the earliest and rarest of the patterns and pepper and salts decorated this way were sold through Primavera in the mid 1950s. The vinegar bottle is decorated in the most often used pattern. Vinegar bottles decorated this way were also sold with the cat pepper and salts illustrated on the previous page. The pattern on the salt on the right side was the last pattern introduced and could be sold with a pepper decorated in the same pattern as the vinegar bottle in this photograph.

coloured Terra cotta bodies. Other members contribute in various ways to the creative processes which culminate in firings at a very high temperature'.

The use of the term 'terra cotta' is strange because the Pottery did not produce any items made from terra cotta. However, their early wares were not fired to the very high temperature necessary for porcelain because of the problems Richard had when designing the kilns and as a result many of Susan's sculptures look as if they were made from terra cotta but in fact they were not, they were made in stoneware. And so it is thought that early tableware probably looked similar in colour to terra cotta, hence the description in the Pottery's catalogue.

Tableware

The Pottery only started producing tableware on a regular basis in 1955 but it was never made in any quantity because it could not be produced at a price that compared favourably with the output of the large potteries at Stoke-on-Trent. Large scale production was dependent on having a jigger and batting machine in order to make plates and Richard and Susan could not afford to buy the jigger until 1955 when the business had grown in size. Prior to this Richard had thrown some mugs, but the porcelain they used was not sufficiently plastic, making it difficult to throw them on the wheel. So Richard tried moulding them in various ways. He first tried to slip cast some cups but they did not seem very satisfactory, possibly because the clay drew away from the mould as it dried, and so in the end they were 'jollied' using the jigger and bat. Similarly the handles were 'pulled' to start with, but later a mould was made and the handles were slip cast. Susan remembered that when Bernard Leach visited the Pottery he was absolutely horrified to see that they used a jigger and bat. As far as he was concerned this went totally against the ethos of handcrafted pottery. The photograph on page 13 shows an early hand-thrown Parkinson Pottery cup, saucer and jug. The throwing rings can clearly be seen on the jug in the photograph, as can Richard's impressed mark. These pieces made around 1954 with their 'line and squiggle' decoration were produced in two different colour ways, either yellow iron, blue-grey and green black, or, pink, yellow and red iron. The Pottery also made porridge bowls and lidded soup bowls in various designs of yellow iron, green-black and blue-grey.

Above: The large cricketer, model number 72, 15 inches high.

Different potteries develop their own characteristic styles. The cups that the Parkinsons designed were sometimes decorated with pairs of vertical lines, as can be seen in the photograph on page 13. The normal method would have been to space the vertical lines equally or to group them in threes, but the Parkinsons chose to group them in pairs going against recognised artistic wisdom. A later, larger version of the cup with chequer decoration can be seen in the photograph on page 43. The chequer pattern was quite widely used in the 1950s and potters such as Wally Cole at Rye Pottery also used it. The large cup is a splendid size to drink from as it holds a generous half-pint of liquid. In addition to this cup the Pottery also produced a very wide shallow cup.

The Pottery made other tableware including bowls of different sizes, vinegar bottles and pepper and salt pots. The first pepper and salt pots, model number 36, were introduced in 1954 and at that date they were decorated with stripes. The catalogue refers to them as *'large'* but in reality they were tall and thin. A very slight variation to the top and body of the mould of the pepper and salt and a slight change of decoration turned them into models of tall cats which were also pepper and salts. These pots are almost identical to models 48 and 49, which are models of two cats known as *small cats* that were made to be sold as a pair. The *cat pepper and salt pots* were introduced around 1955 and were models 64 and 65. To aid identification the salt, which is taller, is usually mostly white in colour and the pepper mainly black. For a few months after their introduction the *cat pepper and salts* had a white *mustard dish* with light flecking to accompany them, which could also be sold with the *large pepper and salt* if required. This dish was usually painted with red iron and so appears brown in colour rather than the normal black. This was done deliberately to create a colour contrast. The *mustard dish*, however, was not in production for very long before being withdrawn. The reason for this was that the dish, which was oval with two pointed ends, had to be slip-cast and as a consequence was rather slow to make and hence costly. In addition the purchasers seemed to want a covered bowl for mustard rather than an open dish and so the *mustard pot*, number 105 was introduced later. The *cat pepper and salt* could also be bought with a tall oil or vinegar bottle, model number 63, which would also accompany the *large pepper and salt* if required.

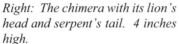

Left: The dragon with its rather stubby wings. 3 inches high.

Right: The chimera with its lion's head and serpent's tail. 4 inches high.

The *small pepper and salt*, model number 60, was introduced just before the *cat pepper and salt*. They are shorter and squatter than the earlier pots and appear to have sold very well. They were probably more stable than the taller version and they were also considerably cheaper, for example in 1961 they were selling for 17/6d a pair when the taller version was selling for 25/-. (£0.875 and £1.25 respectively.) The moulds of the *small and large pepper and salts* and the *vinegar bottles* were eventually sold to Cinque Ports Pottery, Rye and so the same shapes can be found with the Cinque Ports Pottery's backstamp on the base.

Later large models

The *large cricketer* and *large golfer* were first made in 1956, they were introduced because the Pottery was asked for something typically British by buyers from the USA. The *large golfer*, model number 70, is dressed in traditional British golfing clothes, see page 107. The *large cricketer*, model number 72, is very stolid, and was described by Susan as being a 'Cowdrey-like' figure. Both were eventually produced in two sizes, but the smaller versions were not introduced until 1960.

The *policeman*, model number 85, which Susan did not care much for, was also made for the American market. The model is sometimes referred to today as the English bobby or Dixon of Dock Green, because of his 'Jack Warner-like' pose. At that time the Americans were the people who had the money and as a consequence the United States market grew to be a large part of the Pottery's business. The Parkinsons also exported to other countries, such as South Africa, but not in such large quantities. When they sold abroad they had to cope with the export paperwork that was required by the UK government in the 1950s. Eight copies of the form had to be produced, which was a dreadful chore using carbon paper on an old-fashioned typewriter.

Other models

Other smaller models introduced at this time were the *bull*, the *dragon* and the *chimera*, the fabled monster with the head of a lion, body of a goat and a serpent's tail. None of these models appear to have been particularly popular. The *dragon* was first made for a Welsh festival, but the Parkinsons may not have been over keen to market it generally as it was difficult to cast because of its short, stubby wings. Richard requested that Susan design the *chimera* and it may not have sold well because it was not a particularly commercial subject. The model for the *bull*, though not popular when it was produced at the Parkinson Pottery, did prove popular later on when it was produced as a money box by the Cinque Ports Pottery, see page 86. Another small, rare model dating from this time is the *whale*, see page 112. It is unusual because it has colour decoration. *'It was rather a dull shape and needed colour'*, Susan commented.

Susan designed three versions of mermaid. The *large mermaid* was the first model but it did not prove particularly popular and so the *small mermaid*, model number 50, followed quite quickly. She often has rather a mischievous look in her eye, as if she could lead a sailor astray. The final version is *baby mermaid,* which was introduced much later and is model number 121. She is rather a chubby little creature and proved to be the most successful of the three models; she also had the added advantage of being made in a simple two-piece mould. The three different mermaid models are illustrated on page 66.

The *folly*, illustrated on page 99, was designed for Michael Trevor Williams who had been in the Royal Green Jackets in the Second World War and had been a friend of Susan's from that time. After the War he became a chef at the Berkeley and the Savoy hotels. By the time he requested the *folly* he was the manager of the Portmerion Hotel situated in the fantasy Welsh village of the same name. He lived nearby in Deudraeth Castle, which also held his collection of contemporary art. The *folly* is a strange model in that it is quite different from Susan's normal style of work, as it does not rely on fine black and white decoration to create interest on the surface of the model. Instead two colours, brown and green-black were used in its decoration, which is naturalistic in style. Only a small number of models were made from the *folly* mould and it is one of the rarer Parkinson models.

The teapot pictured in the photographs on page 105 is unique. It was made one day for a bit of fun, probably because there was some slip left in the bucket at the end of the day. It is known as *Nellie teapot* and, as can be seen from the base, all the workers helped in making it, including Susan who has put her initials under the handle next to the drawing of a cat. Inside, on the base of the pot, is a picture of Colin's bubble car, which was infamous because it had no reverse gear so that it could be driven on a motorbike licence. This meant that it had to be manhandled if reverse was required! The bubble car was used to take *all* the pottery workers to the local shop on rare occasions in the summer to buy ice creams.

Working at the Pottery
The conditions at the Pottery, as at most potteries, were not always good. They were generally either too hot or too cold. In the winter it got very cold and the concrete floors did not help to warm the building. Sitting still for hours while fettling and decorating meant getting chilblains despite the oil stove, but the stove was good for heating up cans of soup which were a welcome hot lunch for those who lived too far away to cycle home at lunchtime. Those that stayed enjoyed playing ping pong in the shed during the lunch break, possibly to warm up. Michael Parkinson, Richard's cousin, who stayed for a while at the Pottery introduced this activity.

Ann recalled that in the winter she would often decorate with Susan's French bulldog, Beetle, curled up asleep on one of her feet. This way they both kept warm. Ann left in 1958 when she married, as she and her husband moved to Newchurch, Romney Marsh. But she soon missed the Pottery and the camaraderie and so after a few months she returned to work part-time, travelling from Newchurch on a moped. Both Ann and Jean thought it was one of the happiest times of their lives and their friendship has lasted over the years. There were occasional trips out which probably helped to create a bond; in particular the Farnborough Air Show became a regular annual outing and all the Pottery staff went.

The Parkinson's flat, which was above the kiln must have been very cosy when the kiln was being fired. It was decorated in typical avant-garde style for the late 1950s with black and red walls and black and white stencilled curtains, and the chaise-long in the lounge was propped up with a couple of books.

Above: A close-up of a pawn on an 8¾ inch plate from the chess series, which was originally made for an exhibition in the USA. Original photograph by Henry Lewes.

CHAPTER 4   SCULPTURE, EXHIBITIONS AND THE AMERICAN MARKET

The Circle and The Square 1951

The first exhibition at which Susan's work was shown was held in London in 1951 near Bond Street. It was called *The Circle and The Square* and was sponsored by the Council of Industrial Design. The Council was set up to help Britain's industrial sector adapt to peace time conditions and to promote the use of innovative methods and materials. Their first exhibition *Britain Can Make It,* which was held in 1946, was a great success. *The Circle and The Square* was organised by the Artists' International Association (AIA), a rather revolutionary international group with a left-wing orientation. Susan's exhibits included the Canteen Woman, see page 12. Susan's sculptures and the Pottery's early models were displayed at several other exhibitions during the early 1950s. One of the more important exhibitions for the Pottery itself was one held in Holland as this was where the ceramic models of the *sheep* and the *large dog*, Beetle, were first shown.

Sculpture at Brabourne Lees

Running the Pottery severely restricted the amount of time Susan had available to devote to her own work, in particular producing sculpture for exhibitions. Nevertheless she continued to produce a certain amount of sculpture throughout the 1950s, often working on drawings and ideas between the hours of 1 and 4 am while she was watching the kiln. Richard built a studio in the oast house above the kiln so that she had a space of her own with a good quality of light in which to work during the day. He put in a window that gave a beautiful light as well as a lovely view, making it a really good space in which to work. He also had to floor the room but unfortunately it was not easy to find good timber after the Second World War. Eventually he found a source of oak planks in Tenterden but the wood was green and began to warp when it was laid. The kiln beneath the new studio floor was soon being fired several times a week and the heat caused the planks to shrink leaving large gaps and making the room quite dangerous. When it became impossible to work there Richard converted the 'ping pong' shed into a studio for Susan by putting in a large skylight.

Top of the page: The judge introduced for the American market. Model number 87, 12 inches high.

Susan made the original sculptures of the schoolgirls in the early 1950s while Richard was still developing and improving the kilns. The coke kiln they were using at the time did not reach the required temperature for stoneware. It only heated to the temperature required for earthenware, and as a result, Susan remembered its output was a very peculiar colour! Nevertheless the sculptures of the schoolgirls were considered good enough to be exhibited at Primavera in 1955.

The size of the early coke kiln was another technical limitation Susan had to cope with. When she made the sculpture of the *walking cat*, illustrated on page 100, she had to make the tail slightly shorter than she would have liked so that the sculpture fitted into the kiln. The small stylised head and the long, flexible body of this cat clearly illustrates one of Susan's traits, which is to exaggerate one aspect or feature at the expense of others. Commenting on her technique when modelling this cat, Susan said: '*one tries to see what is important and select that, leaving out what is unimportant and really exaggerating what is very important*'.

Susan created her sculpture of the *tall cat* as soon as Richard had completed the new 4 foot kiln in 1952 just because she wanted to make a large sculpture that would utilise the space. The original sculpture of the cat was very tall, much taller than the ceramic model; it was probably at least 3½

Above: A plate from the chess series decorated with a knight. Part of a publicity photograph taken circa 1957. A plate with a different style of knight is illustrated on page 108.

Left: A close-up of a plate from the chess series decorated with a king. Part of a publicity photograph taken circa 1957.

feet and so it just fitted into the kiln. Susan recalled that the sculpture was very heavy and it was a real struggle for both of them to lift it and put it into the kiln without causing any damage. However, they got it in satisfactorily and it also came out in good shape. Like the large sculpture of the *caged bird*, the *tall cat* was never exhibited because of its size. Nevertheless it proved to be one of Susan's most important sculptures because it was the forerunner of the ceramic model which became one of the Pottery's most prestigious and widely recognised models.

Primavera 1955

Primavera held regular exhibitions of the work of promising artists in all fields at their premises in Sloane Street, London. Susan's sculpture was exhibited there under her maiden name of Sanderson, as was all of her own work. She continued to use her maiden name for her sculpture because Henry Rothchild, who had exhibited her work for a number of years, was keen that she should do so. The 1955 exhibition at Primavera, entitled *Ceramic Texture*, was a joint one with another young ceramic artist, Waistel Cooper. Among Susan's exhibits were the original sculptures of the schoolgirls and several rather stylised bulls and their cows. The bulls were very small models, no more than 6 inches long, quite unlike the large pieces she had been making a year or two previously and more convenient for showing. They were a key part of Susan's exhibits at Primavera and were featured on the cover of the promotional material. Their bodies were made of solid clay and were formed by rolling out flat horizontal platforms of clay to which the legs and head were attached. An idea of what they were like can be obtained from the drawing on the front of the invitation to the preview, illustrated on page 108. The bulls have very elongated features, especially their horns; the exaggerated features and the emphasis on the texture of the clay itself are reminiscent of Susan's sculpture of the dachshund, see page 99. The literature that accompanied the exhibition stated: *'Susan Sanderson studied sculpture at the Royal College of Art, specialising in sculptured pieces influenced by Tanagra figures'*. Tanagra figures were brown madder, terra cotta models and statuettes found at Tanagra, Greece dating from 600 to 300 BC. When asked recently, Susan commented that she did not know where the concept of 'Tanagra' had come from and that it sounded rather pompous! Apart from sculptures, Susan also exhibited several hand-built dishes and similar objects at the *Ceramic*

Texture exhibition and she was particularly proud when the well-known potter, Katherine Pleydell-Bouverie, bought one of her dishes.

Primavera also sold Parkinson ceramics, including quite humble items of tableware such as the *large pepper and salt*. One such *large pepper and salt* available from Primavera, decorated in quite a distinct style, was illustrated in Daily Mail Ideal Home Book 1957. The flat top of the pepper and salt were white as was the base up to the widest part of the body, the rest of the body was black except for quite broad white vertical stripes, similar to the pepper pot in the photograph on page 50.

Heal's Craftsman's Market 1957
Heals, the London furniture and department store exhibited Parkinson ceramics at their *Craftsman's Market* in March 1957. The reviewer for the *Pottery Quarterly* did not seem to be overly impressed with the Parkinsons' work, as he wrote the following:

'*The industrial-studio ware of Richard Parkinson is a consummate fabric finely bearing the monocromatic brushwork he uses for it and not needing much tonal value. The pieces are rather too well thought out for the taste of many studio potters, who will nevertheless admire the combined restraint of execution and richness of material, for it is a rather more dulcet porcelain both in contour and surface than a great deal of work in this medium. His models display the centrifugal swelling of the thrower (indeed some may have had their origin on the wheel).*'

Perhaps the rather pompous review in the Pottery Quarterly illustrates, above all, how written English has improved over the years! It goes on at length in similar style and possibly says more about the prevailing attitude to what constituted 'good pottery' than Richard Parkinson pottery. The reviewer would appear to prefer the 'dark tenmoko style' of studio pottery that was so popular with potters in

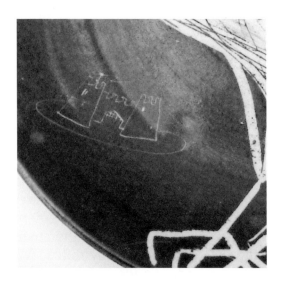

Right: One of the very large plates from the chess series decorated with a rook, 13½ inches in diameter.

Above: A close-up of the dish showing the faint sgraffito castle at the bottom left of the plate which is attached to the rook's left leg by a chain.

Right: Greek head, model number 67, 13 inches high.

the late 1950s, and it is perhaps typical of the period that well thought-out pieces could be condemned as not being immediate or spontaneous enough.

But the reviewer must have been reasonably impressed as he continues: '...*the humour of the models is very genuine; considered perhaps but never calculated.... Also displayed on this pleasing stall in the market were cups and saucers and plates and pieces individually made and decorated by the principal, for Richard Parkinson is not a mere designer, like many who approach pottery using similar methods, but a real potter who is unlikely to turn to designing packaging at the first ill wind. If the gap between factory and studio can be bridged, here is a downright healthy way of doing it.*'

The conflict between mass production and hand crafted work raged for many years throughout the 1950s and up to the 1970s and a number of potteries tried, fairly unsuccessfully to bridge the gap between factory and studio. The Parkinsons went completely against the current thinking of the time when they decided to make porcelain sculptures. This was either quite a brave or foolhardy thing to do. The 1950s saw the work and ideas of a few pre-war potters, in particular Bernard Leach, being accepted and copied by the majority. Stoneware became very popular and some of it was very thick and chunky and most of it was tableware or other functional ware covered in thick, dark glazes. The Parkinson's pieces were quite the opposite, they were generally not functional and the style was light because of the material used, the style of decoration employed and above all the humour incorporated in the piece. Also, the studio pottery of the 1950s had to be made entirely by hand if it was to be considered 'real' studio pottery. Susan recalled an occasion when Bernard Leach came to visit and wandered around in rather a grand way, probably because he did not really approve of the Parkinsons' methods. Richard's view, which seems very sensible, and was one that Susan agreed with, was that if a machine could do something quicker, cheaper and better than the hand, then it should be employed. This would then enable the handwork to be put into wherever it counted. During his visit, Bernard Leach told them a story about his pottery and work which ended '*and so I just picked it up and threw it in the slops*' and this became a standard Parkinson expression or joke so that '*throw it in the slops*' was often uttered when something had gone wrong.

Chess tableware made for a touring exhibition in the USA

The chess series was a range of tableware that was initially created for the USA. Susan designed the range for an exhibition, which was to tour the United States. The organising group had asked for something special and so she designed a complete set of stunning tableware. It included a very large plate or dish, 14 inches across, which was usually decorated with a rook, a rather menacing looking bird, which had a small castle attached to its leg, emphasising its connection with chess. The range comprised six standard size dinner plates, 8¾ inches in diameter in those days, each plate in the set was decorated differently, with: a king, queen, rook, bishop, knight or pawn. These were not depictions of chess pieces but portraits of the characters. There were also six small, squared, white side-plates, 6 inches across that were made to be used as side plates with a dinner setting of the larger chess set plates. They could also be matched with a tea set comprising chequer board cups that had four by four rows of squares in chequer fashion, an example can be seen on the shelf in the photograph on page 43. The chess cups rested on plain black saucers. Finally there were 7½ inch diameter tea plates that were decorated with four black and four white squares surrounding a white square. The white square in the centre was decorated with a sgraffito chess piece, such as white knight or pawn, as on page 57. This tableware is very rare today, as very few sets were made because they were very time-consuming to make and were therefore very expensive to buy; but they must look very striking if a full set is laid on the table.

Neiman Marcus, USA

Neiman Marcus, the well-known department store that started in Dallas, Texas, occasionally ran special cultural celebrations focusing on a particular country. Stanley Neiman, who took over the store in the 1920s, was particularly keen on fashion and design. In 1938 he instigated the *Award for Distinguished Service in the Field of Fashion*, which was awarded over the years to designers including Coco Chanel and Miuccia Prada. In 1957 he started an annual celebration of different countries' cultures and design contributions. Perhaps he had seen or read about Susan's *chess* tableware made for the touring exhibition, in any case he asked Susan to provide some 'heads' for a *British month*. Susan's work was to be displayed in the window of the store and the company requested that she make portrait heads that were typically British. Thinking about what the Americans would consider particularly British, she came up with *'wigs'* as a theme and produced the heads of the *barrister*,

Right: The cavalier, another of the 'wig' models made for the American market. Model number 109. Height 13 inches. In Colin's collection.

61

Above left: Policeman bottle stopper, 4¾ inches long from the top of helmet to the bottom of the cork. Note the initials SP, on the badge on the helmet.
Above right: Short hat, or French gendarme, model number 127, total length 4¾ inches.
Bottom left: Tall hat, or grenadier guard, model number 128, total length 4¾ inches.
Bottom right: Helmet, or cavalry officer, model number 129, total length 4¾ inches.

All apart from the policeman were originally designed by Guy Neale.

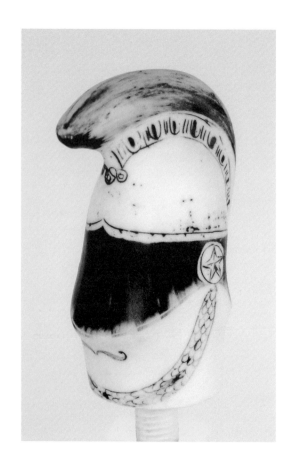

Two bottle stoppers: The bird, model number 92, 4 inches long including the cork, and the fish, model number 97, 4¼ inches long including the cork.

model number 86, and the *judge*, model number 87. Both models have very disdainful expressions on their face. This theme was later supplemented by the addition of a *cavalier* with a curly wig, model number 109. Susan made the cavalier rather dissolute looking with lines under his eyes and he bares a strong resemblance to Charles II. Apart from buying a large number of heads, Neiman Marcus also took a number of the Pottery's *large cats* as well as other items over the years.

Susan had previously made other heads. The first of these were two small classical heads, known as *classical head male and classical head female*, perhaps a Roman emperor and his *'very moral lady'*, see the photograph on page 32. These models, numbers 42 and 43, are approximately 7½ inches high and were always sold as a pair. When the *small classical heads* were sold to the USA the nipples of the lady were not painted as, apparently, the Americans were rather prudish about this! The next head Susan made was the large *Greek head* with his wreath of laurel leaves, model number 67, illustrated on page 59. *'These heads were not particularly British'*, Susan explained, *'but were the sort of thing that the British liked at the time'*. The large size heads, which are about 13 inches high, were expensive to purchase and by 1961 they were selling for £5.25. The *small classical heads* sold for £2 each. The reason for the very high price in the case of the large heads, such as the *Greek head* and the *judge*, was that they took up a lot of space in the kiln and firing the kiln to such a high temperature was the major cost in running the Pottery.

Other wares for the USA

The Pottery was also asked to make bottle stoppers by American buyers, again they wanted something typically British. Susan created the *bird bottle stopper* and the *fish bottle stopper* neither of which could be said to be particularly British, but then she designed the *policeman bottle stopper* (policeman's head) and the policeman's gloved hand indicating 'stop' (known at the Pottery as the *closed hand*). The policeman's gloved hand bottle stopper should not be confused with the large model the *hand in glove* pictured on page 106. The *closed hand bottle stopper* also formed a set with the *open hand bottle stopper*, often referred to as the waving or drowning hand, and the *foot bottle stopper*. The foot and two hand bottle stoppers are illustrated on page 109, where they are either left white or are decorated all over in the normal greeny-black colour. They were also occasionally decorated with a plain glaze of yellow, pale blue or turquoise; these are Briglin and not Parkinson glazes. The bottle stoppers were obviously appreciated generally as the Pottery received a UK commission to make a set of three *policeman* bottle stoppers, which were to be presented to Jack Warner when he left the popular, long-running TV programme, *Dixon of Dock Green.*

Later Susan extended the range by incorporating Guy Neale's bottle stoppers of military heads, the gendarme, grenadier guard and cavalry officer. Susan produced new moulds for these heads and decorated them in the typical Pottery style; the models Guy made a year or so earlier were decorated in red iron and so can easily be identified. The three models Susan made are referred to in the catalogue as *short hat, tall hat* and *helmet,* and are model numbers 127 to 129. The reason for the change in name seems to be that Richard and Susan were unclear which specific type of officer they were modelled on and so played safe by calling them something quite different. Or perhaps if they were selling them mainly to the American market they would not have been able to identify the different uniforms or helmets for reordering purposes.

The *schoolboy,* model number 107, was yet another model that was particularly designed for the American market. Susan tried to present the model as a typical English schoolboy, *'stiff, uniformed and glum'* and he does look a rather well fed, stolid and unresponsive character.

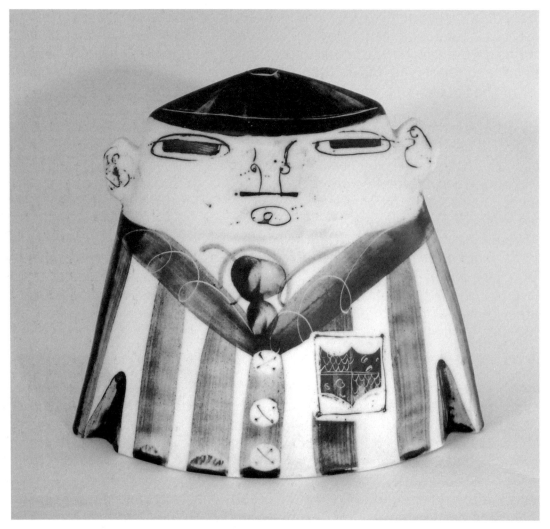

Left: A matt version of the schoolboy money box designed for the American market. Model number 107, 6½ inches high. The hole for the money is a horizontal slot at the back at the base of the cap.

Above left: Small mermaid, model number 50, height 4 ½ inches. In the collection of John Lejeune.

Above right: Baby mermaid, model number 121, 2½ inches high. In the collection of John Lejeune.

Left: Large mermaid, height 9 inches. The earliest of the three mermaid models.

Left: The first model in the theatrical figures series, Sir Laurence Olivier as Henry V. Height 12½ inches. Signed inside the base by Susan: 'Made for Briglin Pottery by Susan Parkinson'.

Opposite page: The cover of the 1959 brochure promoting the figures, illustrating the same model. The brochure was printed was black and cerise.

CHAPTER 5   THEATRICAL FIGURES 1959

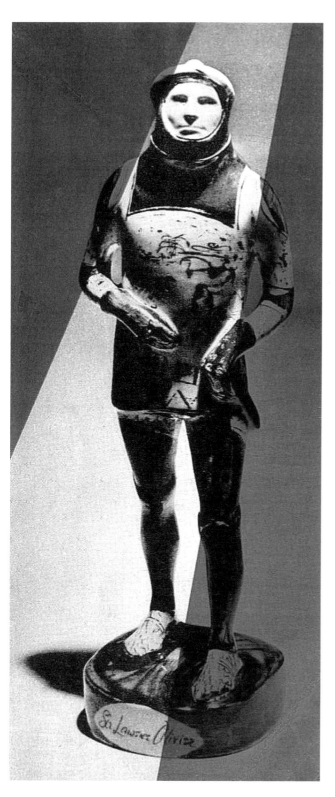

The connection with Briglin Pottery

In the late 1950s the Parkinsons began to use plain coloured glazes on some small items. This was due to a connection with Briglin Pottery, a London based pottery that had been founded by Brigitte Appleby and Eileen Lewenstein in 1948. Richard met Brigitte and Eileen at some stage during the 1950s while he was marketing Parkinson Pottery and as a result of the meeting they agreed to work together on certain projects. This resulted in Briglin Pottery sending the Parkinsons some of their glazes to try out and use. The glazes they supplied were bought-in products, which just required water to be added, in shades of yellow, egg-shell blue, turquoise and a dark greeny-blue. Susan considered the colours to be 'dead' and they certainly did not work well on the Parkinsons' porcelain body as they had been designed for the type of body Briglin used, which was terra cotta. However, Susan used them to a limited extent, mainly on small items such as the *foot* and the *open* and *closed hand bottle stoppers* where detailed black and white decoration was not required.

The Briglin glazes were also used on several items the Pottery made that were connected with gliding. One of these was a dish made for the *National Gliding Championship* held in 1959, in which Richard competed. The mould for this dish was engraved, which leaves the design and lettering raised on the ceramic dish itself. The dish, which is 5 inches long, is the typical pointed oval shape that Susan designed, and is similar in shape to the '1961' dish on page 81. The *Gliding World Championships* took place in the UK in the following year and Richard and Susan made a small number of dishes to sell amongst the pilots. This dish is similar in shape and design to the *National Gliding Championship* dish and bears the embossed words *'British Team 1960 World Gliding Championship'*. Susan recalled that, in this case, they jollied and biscuit fired the dishes before taking them to Briglin where they were glazed and fired. A similarly shaped dark blue dish was also made for the Montacute Motor Museum, but instead of engraving an applied transfer was used for the lettering.

Susan used several of the bright Briglin colours together when she received an order for dishes for Antigua. She painted the dishes with simple brush strokes that represented palm trees and beaches. The word *Antigua* was then scratched through the glaze.

Setting up the theatrical figures project

Brigitte Appleby's partner was the actor Herbert Lom. He had recently taken the leading role in the *'King and I'* in a London theatre and had starred in a number of films including *'The Lady Killers'*. Herbert Lom had the idea that Briglin Pottery should make a series of ceramic figures of famous actors and actresses. They would be modelled playing one of their well-known stage roles just as actors, such as David Garrick and Sarah Siddons, had been in the Georgian era.

Unfortunately Briglin Pottery could not make the figures because it used an earthenware body that was unsuitable for such detailed work. So in 1958 Herbert Lom, who lived close to Brabourne Lees at Lombery Farm, contacted the Parkinsons to ask whether they would make models of seven different theatrical personalities dressed in the costume of one of their well-known roles. The seven actors, who were to be portrayed this way, in the order in which they were to be produced, were:

> Sir Lawrence Olivier as Henry V
> Vivien Leigh as Cleopatra
> Sir John Gielgud as Hamlet
> Dame Margot Fonteyn as Ondine
> Paul Robeson as Othello
> Maria Callas as Violetta
> Sir Alec Guinness as himself

The Parkinsons agreed to design seven models which were to be about 12 inches high, to make the moulds and then to produce and decorate 100 figures from each mould, for a fee of £2 per figure. Once this was agreed Herbert Lom contacted the actors to obtain their permission, which was duly given.

The project was very prestigious and helped to raise the profile of Briglin Pottery and enhance its reputation. The actors were obviously pleased to be included judging by the quotes given in the advertising brochure which promoted the models.

'I do think it is a most marvellous idea, and it is curious that there should be such a gap since the Victori-

Above: The second model in the series, Vivien Leigh as Cleopatra. 12½ inches high.

ans produced figures.   All my very best wishes for your project.'   VIVIEN LEIGH

'I am very honoured to be included in the list of forthcoming portrait figures.'
DAME MARGOT FONTEYN

'I am intrigued to hear about the pottery idea and am delighted to give permission to 'do' me.'
SIR LAURENCE OLIVIER

'Delighted, of course – though what I may look like in pottery is a new hazard.'
SIR ALEC GUINNESS

The cover of the brochure promoting the figures was printed in cerise and black and explained the venture this way:

'Under the Sponsorship of Herbert Lom BRIGLIN POTTERY present great artists of stage and screen in a first edition of porcelain figures designed by Susan Parkinson each figure being 12 ins. in height and hand decorated, price 10 guineas.

'A fine old tradition revived
'We are proud to revive a tradition going back to the middle of the 18th century.   Such notable firms as Bow, Chelsea, Wedgwood and Worcester – and many Staffordshire potters known and unknown – have left us a legacy of clay and porcelain figures representing great theatrical personalities of the past.   Among these great figures were Sarah Siddons, David Garrick, Edmund Kean, Charles Macready and Jenny Lind. It is our aim to add to-day's outstanding performers to this gallery of fame.

'Perfection in miniature
'In reviving a dying art we are striving for perfection in miniature.   The Briglin figures capture the characters and features of some of the best-loved artistes of our time with wonderful delicacy of workmanship and subtlety of style. They are miniature works of art at remarkably reasonable price.

'Dedicated to fame
'In submitting these figures to the audiences of to-day's theatre and concert hall, Briglin Pottery add a humble dedication – to the achievement

Above: Sir John Gielgud as Hamlet. 12½ inches high.

and lasting fame of the outstanding men and women who have consented to be represented in this gallery of the potter's art.

'Our sponsor

'When I was asked to sponsor this new venture I responded immediately and enthusiastically. Immediately because of my love of the theatre, and enthusiastically because of my great interest in well-designed pottery of every age. These new portraits are not only good pottery and good sculpture - they are first class theatre.   *Herbert Lom*

Technical difficulties

Susan set about making the models, which she did either from photographs or real life. Her aim was to capture a movement, a stance, or some mannerism that was individual to each actor so that the public would instantly recognise the likeness in the model. For example, one of the traits she noticed when modelling Sir Laurence Olivier, the first model she tackled, was the way his body came forward and his left foot turned inward. Two of Sir John Gielgud's characteristics that Susan chose to illustrate were his tendency to bend his knees and put his head forward.

Rather appropriately Vivien Leigh followed the model of her husband, Sir Laurence Oliver, in order of production. Susan went to meet her at one of the London theatres not long before Vivien died. She was seated in a reclining pose in the semi-dark, as the curtains were drawn, but Susan remembered that she was very well preserved and she scarcely looked older than her late twenties. Susan said she found it very difficult to produce realistic figures in terms of height that would appear to be a set when displayed together. This was because Vivien Leigh was very petite and, of course, Paul Robeson was quite the opposite.

The project also posed several technical problems. The first was that the moulds had to be made in many pieces because the figures had to be very detailed in terms of facial features, etc. For example Olivier required an eight-piece mould. But the main problem was that the figures with the exception of Paul Robeson and Vivien Leigh had to be relatively tall and thin. This meant the models were quite different to the Pottery's normal production. As the porcelain had to be fired to a very high temperature the tall thin models became rather unstable when the temperature approached 1300°C. *'Olivier often wandered in the kiln and Gielgud always moved as well'*, Susan recalled. This meant that some of the figures came out of the kiln slightly skewed or warped. Jean remembered that the theatrical figures were also very difficult to pack satisfactorily in the kiln. This was because they had to be packed at a slight angle in order to attempt to compensate for their natural tendency to wilt and move a particular way at high temperatures. Eventually Richard purchased a band-sander in order to grind the bases of any models that had warped so that the figures would stand vertically. Overall the wastage was about 50%, which obviously added considerably to their cost.

Every figure stood on a deep, hollow base that bore the name of the actor and the role the actor was playing. Lom was not keen on the Richard Parkinson Pottery name being associated with the project, but Susan was allowed to sign the pieces on the inside of the base. This she did by brushing a band of colour on the white clay and scratching through the colour. She wrote *'Made for Briglin Pottery by Susan Parkinson'*. Each model also has a number between 1 and 100 in Roman numerals inside the base but these numbers cannot be relied on, as one or two numbers may be missing or duplicated because of the kiln disasters. Some figures had to be remade and were given the numbers of the faulty figures they were replacing and, assuming records were not always kept properly, there may even be one or two with the same number!

The decoration on the figures may vary slightly from model to model as they were individually decorated by either Susan or Ann and it took some time to complete because of the detailed work required for areas such as the delicate chain mail that Olivier wears. In terms of production, Sir John

Gielgud was the third model Susan created, followed by Dame Margot Fonteyn and lastly Paul Robeson. The project stopped at this point and probably only about 6 models of Paul Robeson were made, rather than the promised 100.

Half way through the project the Parkinsons realised that they could not make the models for the agreed price of £2, and so they asked Herbert Lom to pay another 5 shillings. He was furious and arrived at the Pottery, with several lawyers, brandishing the contract the Parkinsons had signed. He told them it would be marvellous for them to be able to say that they had made these figures when they came to write their autobiographies! Unfortunately the Parkinsons had more pressing worries than their autobiographies and so, when Lom declined to raise the price, they sadly had to discontinue production. Susan said that she was quite thankful in some ways that the project was halted, because she had no idea how she was going to portray Sir Alec Guinness as *'he had such a rubber face'*. That is to say, he was a very skilful actor who managed to lose his own personality in the character he was playing and as he was the one actor to be modelled as 'himself' he would have been very difficult to depict.

The display at the Design Centre

Despite the termination of the project the figures were displayed at the Design Centre in 1959, where they were on offer for 10 guineas each or 40 guineas the set, which presumably included the fifth and final figure, Paul Robeson. The Duke of Edinburgh went to the opening and bought a set, as did the American actor, Charlton Heston. Judging by the difference between the cost price to Briglin Pottery and the retail-selling price of the models, the Parkinsons were rather hard done by when Herbert Lom refused to increase the price. Nevertheless, the figures are some of the finest that the Richard Parkinson Pottery produced. Susan captured the likenesses of the celebrities remarkably well and the decoration was very detailed and fine. It is perhaps unfortunate that Richard and Susan did not get any credit for the work, as their business would have benefited from consequential orders. Neither did they get any of the glory, as it was Brigitte Appleby who went to Vivien Leigh's dressing room at the New Theatre to present her with the figures of herself and her husband, Sir Laurence Olivier.

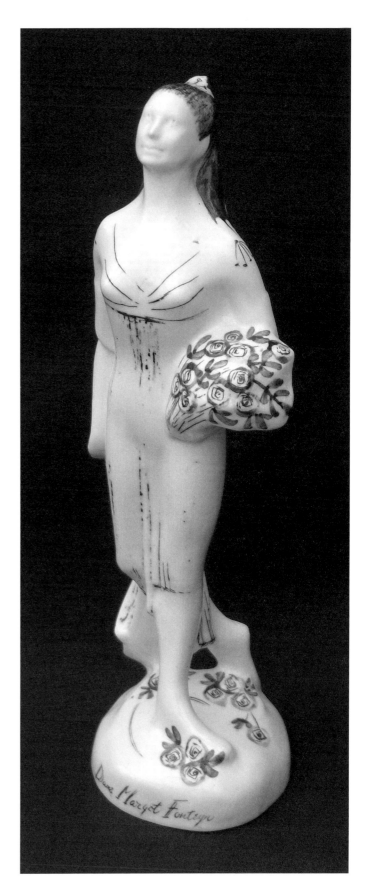

Above: Dame Margot Fonteyn as Ondine. 12 inches high.

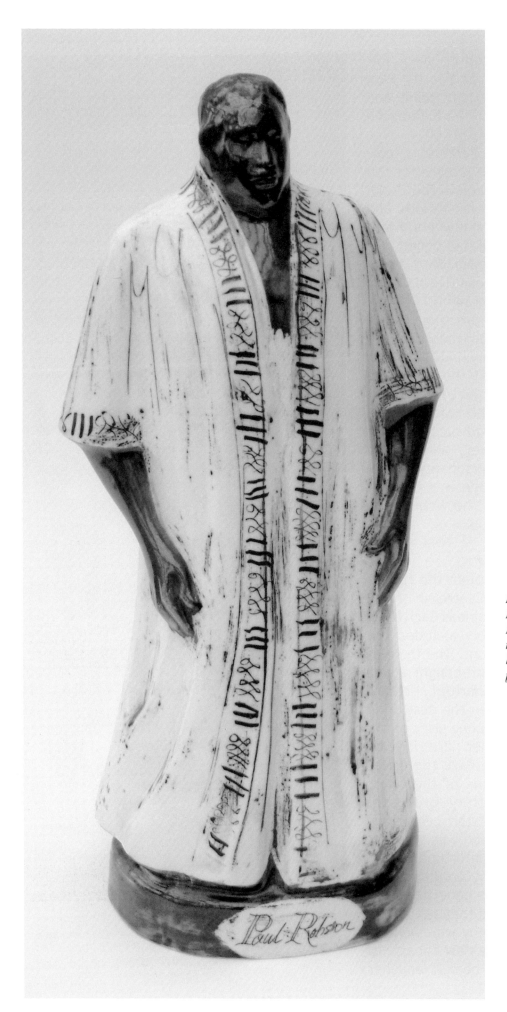

Left: The final theatrical model, Paul Robeson as Othello. 13 inches high. The Parkinsons only completed about 6 ceramic models of Robeson before they broke the contract because of the cost of production.

CHAPTER 6   THE POTTERY 1959 - 61

Small models for gift shops

By the late 1950s the UK economy was beginning to pick up following the Second World War and the Parkinsons started to supply fancy goods shops that were largely catering for the holiday and tourist trade. The model that led them in this direction was the *mouse*. It is model number 71 and was created in 1956 because one of the Pottery's outlets was in the Cornish fishing village of Mousehole, and so it seemed natural for Susan to produce a model of a mouse for this particular outlet. The *mouse* proved a great success in all markets but, naturally, it was especially popular in Mousehole and the shop gave the Parkinsons many repeat orders. There are two colour versions of the mouse, one decorated so that the *mouse* appears black and the base white and the other is reversed with a white *mouse* and a black base. If there are more white mice today it is probably because they were easier to decorate, as it was easier to paint the liquid wax on to the body and scratch the detail through. As a consequence, if the order did not specify the colour, white ones were supplied. If the Pottery received an order for, say, 50 mice from Mousehole, it could be put through the production process without advanced planning because the mice were small and fitted in the kiln easily. Orders for larger pieces meant that Susan had to work out a schedule for the kiln. Mice would also be made if the decorators had a spare hour at the end of the day, and so although it was not an early model it is probably the most common. The mice were made in a long two-piece mould which made five individual mice at a time. Not all the mice are identical in shape, presumably this is because the five

Above: Three versions of the mouse, model number 71, 1¾ inches high. Notice the slightly different shape especially around the ears.

Left: The money cat, with it's stripey decoration, model number 106, 2½ inches high.

Above left: King Canute, model number 100, 4½ inches high. Unfortunately the top of his trident is missing.

Above right: The electric coffee pot, the lid and fitting are missing, 8 inches high. In the collection of John Lejeune.

individual moulds were slightly different or perhaps it is due to fettling differences. The variation can be seen in the photograph on the previous page, where one of the white mice seems to have larger ears and a slightly different profile.

Susan went on to design a number of little birds for the fancy goods shops. The *small bird or coptic bird*, which was the first model the Pottery made and the *little owl* were already in production. The *robin* and the *wren* quickly followed the *mouse* and are model numbers 74 and 79 respectively. As the gift shop market expanded these birds were followed in 1960 by four other birds: the *square*, *pointed* and *nesting birds* and *bird in cage*, model numbers 143 to 146 respectively.

There were also three small models of nondescript dogs: the *short-legged dog, shaggy dog* and *snooty dog*. In addition models of several breeds of thoroughbred dogs were introduced during 1960: the *corgi, boxer, peke* and *poodle*, model numbers 138 to 141 respectively. The dogs generally proved to be almost as good money-spinners as the mice because people seemed keen to buy models of dogs.

Larger models
Despite concentrating on small models Susan was still designing a few slightly larger models aimed at a more discerning market. One of these is a very rare model, *King Canute,* model number 100. He is sometimes referred to as Neptune and as he holds a trident he could be seen this way, but Susan intended the model to represent King Canute attempting to defy the waves. The *woman knitting*, model number 110, illustrates Susan's sharp eye and gentle sense of humour. The woman sits placidly, with podgy arms and legs and an ample chin that merges into a neck encircled with a string

of pearls, but her sharp eyes would not miss a great deal. Susan also made a model of *women shopping*. '*The women were all sorts of shapes and were rather wide round the hips but they had rather nice shoes*', she remembered. Again both of these models are rare, as they were not made in any great quantity.

Susan also extended the money box range that had first started in the early 1950s with the *money bear*. She added the *money cat,* a stripey cat which is model number 106, the schoolboy, model number 107 and then shortly afterwards the *money pig,* model number 125. All the money boxes apart from the schoolboy seem to have been aimed at the gift shop market.

Other work
In order to help their finances during the late 1950s the Parkinsons began to make industrial items as and when requested to do so.   This obviously grew into a reasonably substantial part of the business because the 1961 catalogue describes the Pottery as '*manufacturers of fine porcelain figures, decorative, useful and industrial ware*'. Susan recalled that they made a range of rather '*sinister medical-shaped dishes*', including a kidney-shaped dish. But the rubber glove format was the earliest and probably the most successful of the industrial items they produced because they were able to adapt this commission and use it as a decorated ceramic model as well. The original was requested

Right: Woman knitting, model number 110, 7½ inches high. In the collection of Barbara McAdam-Seth.

Below: The rear view of the woman knitting (a different model).

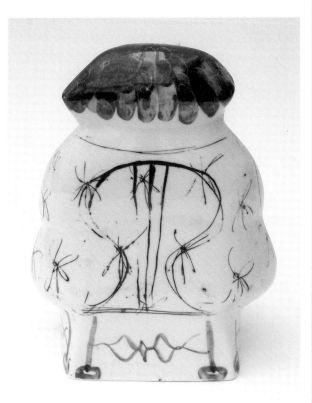

Left: The money pig, model number 125, 4 inches high. Compare this with the Cinque Ports Pottery version on page 111.

Below: Two of the new hedgehogs introduced in 1960, model number 155, 1½ inches high and 3½ inches long.

by the medical supplies company Pfizer which operated nearby in Hythe. They wanted a standard hand for use in the manufacture of surgical gloves. Having produced the model for the hand the Parkinsons used it themselves, and made some decorated models, with for example a chequer pattern design or painted as a tree with birds, the trunk running up the wrist and branching out across the hand and fingers, like veins, this is illustrated on page 106. The model is known as *hand in glove* and was model number 90 in the catalogue, but only a few were decorated more as a joke than a serious production item.

The Parkinsons designed a ceramic coffee machine. Susan recalled that it was not at all easy to design and make as she had to make a ceramic plug that would fit a socket. Because the porcelain they used had a very high shrinkage rate when the clay dried it was very difficult to determine in advance how to achieve an exact fit. The lid of the coffee machine also had to be very precise, with a flat centre part, but why and what the coffee machine was to be used for is no longer known. One of the prototypes minus the lid and fittings is illustrated on page 74. The Pottery also did a certain amount of work for the electronic industry producing strange ceramic objects, which are clearly marked 'RICHARD PARKINSON MADE IN ENGLAND', unlike most of the Pottery's ceramic models.

In addition Susan designed a bowl which was to feature in a TV advertisement for the well-known soup manufacturer, Heinz. It was very tricky to design to their specification as they required a heart-shaped bowl that maintained the heart shape all the way down from the lip to the base of the bowl.

New models for 1961

By 1961 the number of models Susan had created had grown considerably. The models described as new in the 1961 catalogue, issued in January, are:

Model	Model number
Long leaf dish	126
Corgi	138
Boxer	139
Peke	140
Poodle	141
Little owl	142
Square bird	143
Pointed bird	144
Nesting bird	145
Bird in cage	146
Peacock	147
Small cricketer	148
Tennis player	149
Small golfer	150
Big owl	151
Coffee mug	152
Small leaf plate	153
Tall goblet IV	154
New hedgehog	155

Above: The poodle, model number 141, 3 inches high. This model is unusual because surface decoration is used to represent the fur rather than applied colour.

All of the models listed above were presumably designed during 1960. Because so many new models were introduced the range had to be rationalised and in 1961 the following models were described as having been withdrawn. However, they were still available to customers if a specific order was placed:

Model	Model number
Wren	79
Squirrel	99
Little owl	46
Robin	74
Hedgehog	80
Large owl	9
Chorus of birds	32
Small classical heads	42/43
Two cats	33
Golfer	70
Cricketer	72
Triangle dish	35

Below: The peke, model number 140, 2¼ inches high and 4 inches long. In Jean's collection.

Above left: Bird in cage model number 146, 2½ inches high.

Above right: The late, angular, big owl, model number 151. Height 6½ inches and 7½ inches wide. This one is decorated in very similar style, with feathers, to the bird in cage, above, and also to the late little owl with painted feathers, illustrated on page 109. This feather decoration is quite unlike the decoration on either of the earlier owl models.

The *squirrel*, model number 99 and illustrated on page 107, must have been one of the most unpopular models Susan made as it was only in production for a couple of years before being withdrawn. Although the *hedgehog*, model number 80, was also withdrawn in 1961 it was not due to lack of popularity; replacement models for the *hedgehog* and both the *little owl* and *large owl* had been created in 1960 and so the old models were withdrawn, as can be seen from the list on the previous page. The new *hedgehog* is a longer, flatter creature with sharper edges and was decorated with '*better*' stars, according to Susan. The earlier version, illustrated on page 80, has a shorter body and was also often decorated with stars, but all sorts of different decorative styles were tried on the earlier hedgehog.

Susan continued to look back to some of her early work when she designed other new models. For example, *bird in cage* model number 146, is based on the idea Susan conceived when she made the original stoneware model of the *caged bird* in 1951, illustrated on page 14. The rather chirpy porcelain bird with his tuft of feathers is quite different to the original sculpture and his cage is represented by two circular bent canes that fit through holes in the base, instead of the iron rod that had been used on the original. '*It's rather a parakeety type of bird*', Susan commented referring to the porcelain version. This model and many of the later models such as the *small cricketer, small golfer* and *tennis player* were not made in any quantity because the Pottery began to wind down soon after they were introduced.

The *coffee mugs,* introduced in 1961, were made in two designs. The first design was one of a variety of Greek columns, Doric, ionic and Corinthian, as can be seen from the photograph opposite, and the other was the chequer pattern. The *tall goblet*, illustrated page 109, was *'a nightmare to make'*, according to Susan. It has a hollow, circular stem that is very wide at the base but narrows to a very small diameter as it moves upwards, on top of this rests a large horizontal surface that then turns up at almost right angles to form the cup. Because of its narrow mid point and large bowl it was worse than *Olivier* and *Gielgud* in the kiln; *'it bent everywhere'*. As a consequence very few were made.

The Pottery made several 'leaf' plates including the *small leaf plate* that was designed for salad. This was introduced in 1960 but it did not sell well, Susan thought that the reason was probably because it was rather too small for salad; however it seems to have found a market later when the mould was sold to Cinque Ports Pottery. The *long leaf dish* is very long, 3 feet in length and so it only just fitted in the kiln. It is a boat-shaped dish specially designed for flowers or plants and was sold with a metal stand that had very long, thin legs. By the late 1950s new exotic pot plants, such as coleus and rubber plants, and Japanese floral decorations had become popular as interior decoration and the Parkinsons were tapping into this market. Owen Evans, the local blacksmith, made the stands for the *long leaf dishe*s; he lived in nearby Stone Street and had a workshop in Canterbury. He had originally contacted the Parkinsons to ask them to make flowerpots for him, as he had designed and made a number of wrought iron plant holders and needed pots to fit them. Following this Susan designed several plant holders and their collaboration led to Susan designing Owen Evans' metalwork catalogue.

The final models and lustre ware
One of the last things Susan did before the Pottery closed was to experiment with lustre. This work had to be fired in the small kiln rather than the main kiln. When Susan used the large kiln she relied

Above: 1 pint and 1/2 pint tankards and a coffee mug, 1/3 pint, decorated with Doric, ionic and Corinthian columns. They were made during the last year or so of the Pottery's life and are in Colin's collection.

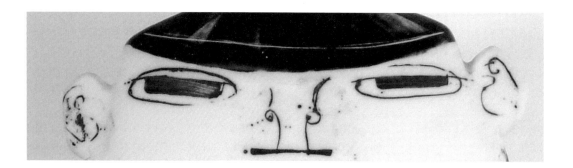

on reduction to achieve the right colour, but lustre ware requires oxygen and it needs to be really oxygenated otherwise it goes hopelessly wrong. Even in the small kiln this could be a problem. Susan chose to use a pink lustre onglaze but only a few models were made with this glaze, mainly the little wren illustrated on page 102.

One of the last models, not included in the January 1961 catalogue because it was designed that year, was the *Driad*. She was *'a large lady'* according to Susan and, of course, part tree. Susan was particularly pleased with this model.

The final piece Susan made at the Pottery was a bust of Sir Winston Churchill. Churchill approved the model not long before he died. Only 5 models were made before the Pottery closed, one of which went to Churchill himself. Susan sculpted the bust in terra cotta and captured Churchill's likeness

Top of the page: The school boy with his rectangular eyes.

Above left: The sheep showing the running pattern of loopy S's.

Above right: The early version of the hedgehog, showing the 'swiss roll' eyes. This model, number 80, was replaced in 1960/61 with the longer slimmer version, also decorated with stars and illustrated on page 76.

and character admirably. The models themselves are plain white except for a black pedestal and are unglazed. Churchill's head is relatively small and is depicted in great detail, but his shoulders are very wide and taper to a small circular pedestal. The resulting effect is of a man of incredible strength. The *Churchill* model is recorded as model number 131 which shows that it was made during 1960, despite this it was the final model to go into production. The reason for the delay in its introduction was that it took some time to cast a model from the mould, send it to Sir Winston and gain his approval for its reproduction.

Susan's style of decoration

Looking back over the body of decorated ware that Susan produced two or three characteristics in her style of decoration become clear, and their identification may help the collector recognise her work if the porcelain is unmarked. One is the way she portrays the eyes of both animals and humans. Animals normally have eyes which are represented by a thin line drawn round in ever-increasing circles, like a swiss roll. This can be seen, for example in the *hedgehog* (on the opposite page), the *mouse* (page 73) and the *squirrel* (page 107). Her human models normally have eyes that are represented by an oval line with a large black rectangle within it, see the *schoolboy* (on the opposite page), *haystack hair* and *pigtails* (page 35), the *large golfer* (page 107) and the *chess king* (page 56).

Another of Susan's characteristic decorating devices is something that looks like the astrological symbol for Aries. This can be seen on the side of the dark *square pig* (page 107) and representing the nose of *pigtails* (page 28). It appears on many of Susan's pieces, including the wing of both the drawing and model of the *small bird* (page 19) where it is inverted. Yet another characteristic is a running pattern of loops that looks rather like a series of loopy letter S's or figure 8's joined together, see the *sheep* (opposite) and the *peacock* (page 106).

Finally there is a device which looks like an elaborate capital letter S and is perhaps her initial. This device is often used to create the tail of the *square pig* (page 90) and is used again to create the curly hair on the ears of the *poodle* (page 77). A different way of identifying Susan's work is to look out for her initials hiding in unlikely places such as the badge on the policeman's helmet on the *policeman* model and bottle stopper (front cover and page 62).

Above: A dish 5 inches long made in 1961 to celebrate the reversible year date.

81

Above: One of the few ceramic models made of Sir Winston Churchill, the Pottery's final production model. 9 inches high and 8 inches wide. In Colin's collection.

Opposite: Susan's terra cotta sculpture of Sir Winston Churchill from which the mould for the Pottery's model was created. Photographed by Henry Lewes.

CHAPTER 7   THE CLOSURE AND AFTERWARDS

Closing the Pottery

One day in 1960, probably because of her qualifications, Susan was contacted by Hornsey School of Art requesting her to teach at the college. As this would mean travelling to London two days a week and being away from the Pottery she discussed it with Richard and they tried to decide which one of them the Pottery could spare most. In the end Richard went to teach at Hornsey in Susan's place and after a short while there he met an art student who was to become his second wife. This meant that he wished to leave the Pottery and move elsewhere.

Without Richard's input Susan could not continue to run the Pottery as the loss of Robert the mould-maker shortly before meant that she was already doing his work as well as her own. Closure would mean that the financial backers would lose most of their investment but Susan felt that she had no choice, as there was no one who could take over Richard's role and so she set about winding the business up. The people who had lent money had to be repaid as far as possible and this meant selling as much of the equipment as could be sold at the best possible price. This included the jolly and wheel, which Colin Pearson, who was working at Aylesford, Kent, bought. The kiln, which was built of very good quality bricks, was sold to Judith Partridge of Rodmell, Lewes, and had to be dismantled brick by brick so that it could be moved and rebuilt at her Pottery.   H. M. Customs and Excise had to be satisfied that trading had ceased and that Susan had not kept any ceramics that could be sold without the payment of purchase tax going into the government coffers. So a purchase tax officer came to watch Susan break the remaining stock and the remaining moulds in front of him. The pottery was smashed in an adjacent field, where, in the past, Colin and Jean had occasionally broken poor quality models that could not be sold as seconds. Pottery shards can still be found coming to the surface of the field today after a particularly wet period. Closing the Pottery took a considerable time, several years, and the company was eventually wound-up on 11th November 1964.

Top of the page: A bronze head of Jemima Johnstone, aged 9 years, 16 inches high. 1980. In the Johnstone family's collection.

Opposite and pages 88, 89 and 96:   Susan's drawings.

Cinque Ports Pottery

Quite a number of the moulds were sold to George Gray of the Cinque Ports Pottery in Rye who hoped to reproduce the ware at his Pottery. George Gray was a marketing man rather than a potter and Susan tried to dissuade him from buying the moulds as the clay bodies they used were so different she was afraid the moulds would be of little use. She went to the Cinque Ports Pottery to do some colour tests, but was not impressed with the resulting models as it was impossible to reproduce the ware precisely as the Pottery did not use a porcelain body. For example, when the *policeman bottle stopper* was made with the Cinque Ports' clay the resulting model was considerably larger than the Parkinson version and therefore out of balance with the normal size bottle. The reason for this was that the clay they used fired at a lower temperature and therefore the model shrank to a lesser extent during firing as less water was driven from the clay. Some idea of the high shrinkage involved with the Parkinsons' porcelain body can be gauged by the length of the two *cow* models made from the same mould: the Cinque Ports' model is 12 inches long and the Parkinson one, only 11 inches. Susan said that when she first started to work with porcelain she found it very difficult to gauge the size the original model needed to be, because of the amount of reduction caused by firing the porcelain body to such a high temperature. But eventually she got used to it and could allow for it accurately.

Cinque Ports Pottery used the earlier version of the *large owl* mould and attempted to decorate it in a similar unglazed style to the Parkinson Pottery, see page 111. The decoration is not of such a high standard and the finish is rather powdery in appearance. The solid black eyes are not at all typical of Parkinson ware and this was the deciding factor when Susan Parkinson determined that the piece in question (although unmarked) was not a test piece made at the Parkinson Pottery but a Cinque Ports Pottery model. (For a comparison of eyes see pages 22 and 24.)

Cinque Ports Pottery appears to have produced only a limited amount of ware from the Parkinson moulds. Their efforts with the decoration of the *large owl* may have led to the abandonment of the black and white colour scheme in favour of a range of different colours. They used two main styles of decoration: a colourful underglaze decoration on a white base and a bluey-grey matt finish brushed roughly over a base of dark brown-black which had been painted with wax swirls and other patterns. Examples of the former style of decoration, which are quite effective, are illustrated on page 111 and the latter on this page. Cinque Ports did not use the same delicate wax resist technique and so their

Left: A Cinque Ports Pottery bull money box, 8 inches long. The patterns were formed by painting swirls and other shapes in wax over a dark brown-black slip, before roughly painting a bluey-grey matt finish over the whole model creating a streaky appearance.

Above: A lead statue of Rufus Johnstone, aged 2½ years, 29 inches high. Circa 1972. In the Johnstone family's collection.

wares can quite easily be identified even if they are not marked on the base. Generally Cinque Ports Pottery did not take the trouble with decoration that Susan and her team had done. For example Susan noticed that when painting the blue colour on the helmet of the *policeman bottle stopper* they did not apply it under the rim of the helmet, so rendering the three-dimensional model rather pointless. The colour underneath the rim emphasises the shape of the helmet that was modelled to stand proud of the head.

George Gray appears to have used the moulds of the *small leaf plate* and the *small pepper, salt and vinegar* in particular. He also used the moulds for the *bull*, *money pig* and *money bear* extensively, and to a lesser degree the moulds for the *large owl* (early version), *cow* and *large pepper and salt*. The nose of the *money pig* was made slightly smaller for ease of moulding at Cinque Ports Pottery. All of the animal models were turned into money boxes if they were not already designed that way. The Cinque Ports Pottery versions have holes with plastic bungs on the underside of the body so that the money can easily be removed. The Parkinson money boxes did not have holes for the extraction of coins. Presumably one was supposed to shake them back through the entry slot, or smash the pot!

Commissions and work after the Pottery closed

After the Pottery closed Susan did all sorts of commissions and a wide variety of work but she did little modelling, except when she was specifically asked. One person who asked her was her cousin, Paul Johnstone. He requested that Susan sculpt a bronze head of his wife, Barbara, and then in due course his three children, see pages 85 and 98. Susan was very struck with the arms of the younger son, Rufus, and so instead of just his head she decided to produce a full-sized statue of him in lead. The lead statue and bronzes were cast at the Art Bronze Foundry in London.

One of Susan's first commissions was to make a soup ladle for Knorr, the Swiss company who made packet soups. They wanted a ladle for a TV advertisement that would look like an eighteenth century, elaborate, ceramic ladle with gilt decoration. But they could not find one that would do in an antique shop or anywhere else and so they contacted the Pottery to see if one could be made. By this time the Pottery had closed but Susan said that she would make it anyway. She modelled it in fibreglass which she painted to look like

porcelain with beautiful gilt scrolls, and she also painted 'Knorr' on it in large letters that would be visible to television viewers. The series of advertisements ran for a couple of years, which was fortunate for Susan as she had to make a number of replacement ladles for the company. Apparently the cameras tended to get very hot and when they were close to the ladle it began to melt, or sometimes an accident occurred and the ladle broke.

By necessity Susan proved quite versatile after the Pottery closed and her design skills branched out in a number of different directions. She designed several items in wood, including a cotton tree whose purpose was to store cotton reels separately in order to stop them getting into a tangled mess. As its name implies the tree had wooden branches, each of which held several cotton reels that were secured with wooden pegs. It proved quite popular, apparently. Then she designed some 'fun things' out of cane, for example an antlered head that could have belonged in an ancestral home.

Susan also designed magazine covers and letterheads. One of the magazine covers she designed was for a chemistry or science magazine, she chose to use a design that was based on the six-sided carbon molecule, which was quite important and easily recognised at the time. The company wanted a design that they could alter from edition to edition, and so Susan did a number of slightly different versions so that the cover could be changed. The design also incorporated coloured circles, the colour of which could also be changed from edition to edition to add variety.

In order to supplement the income from these projects Susan went back to teaching and worked at Maidstone School of Art where she taught life drawing. David Hockney taught engraving at the college at the time and his room was next to Susan's. One day she went to an exhibition of works of art and although she had very little money she saw a picture she felt she had to have, never mind whether she could afford to eat for the next week or not! The picture was a signed limited edition print entitled *'Three Kings and a Queen'* and was priced quite highly at £12. Susan spent her money and brought the picture home feeling very satisfied. Only when she was home did she look at the signature and realise that it was the work of her next-door neighbour at Maidstone College of Art, David Hockney. She cursed herself because she felt sure that he would have given her one free if she had asked!

While Susan was teaching at Maidstone in 1962 she also spent a period driving up to London at night to work on film animation for the TV cartoon *Pugwash*. On these occasions she was very grateful for the company of her French bulldog, Beetle, as the old Citroen she drove frequently boiled over and she spent quite a lot of time sitting in lay-bys waiting for the water to cool, and so Beetle's presence was a great comfort.

Susan also created two splendid dolls houses. One was a very grand dolls house, which was a perfect replica of her cousin, Paul Johnstone's, London house. Not only was the exterior an exact copy, but

Susan also copied everything precisely in the interior of the house, even down to the portrait in oils over the fireplace. The other dolls house was made with the help of Molly Wood. Perran Wood sent his eight-year old daughter, Molly, to Susan because she wanted to learn carpentry. When asked what she wanted to make, Molly said wanted to make a wheelbarrow as a present for her father, but Susan dissuaded her and asked her what pleased her father. *'His house'* she replied, and so Susan and Molly made a model of their rather beautiful London house. Susan recalled that despite her thin, little arms the girl was very determined and did a lot of the sawing and much of the work herself.

During the 1970s Susan designed a series of mobiles for Liberty's of London. They were made from sequins, pearls and bamboo. The mobiles were constructed from two bamboo cane circles from which fish were suspended on fine thread. Sequins were used to represent the scales of the fish and pearls were used to represent the bubbles they blew. Each one involved a considerable amount of work and as Liberty's required quite a number, Susan asked Jean Rogers, who by this time had a family but still lived in Brabourne, to help her with the project.

The bad storm, that swept the country in the autumn of 1987, created a lot of broken glass. Susan thought that she could use this windfall creatively and found that glass was a much easier material to work with than porcelain. *'At 700°C one could open the kiln and look at the pieces, stick a screwdriver in and pull up the glass like treacle'*, she explained. There were also economies and advantages over porcelain as the glass lay flat in the kiln and so more could be fitted in. This started her on a new line of creative work, but she did continue to do a certain amount of painting and modelling.

Brickwood House and The Arts Dyslexia Trust
In 1963 Susan agreed to set up an Art Department at Brickwood House, Northiam, which is near Rye in East Sussex. The head master, Malcolm Richie, was one of the first people in England to recognise dyslexia and turn the school into an establishment where teaching methods could evolve to help dyslexics. Now known as Frewen College it educates dyslexic boys who previously were known as *'difficult boys who could not get on in life'*. *'Everyone else concentrated on what was bad about dyslexics but this school focused on what they could do well'*, Susan commented. She found they were more talented than most of her art students at Maidstone and very rewarding to teach. The Art Department expanded under Susan from the original cowshed into all the buildings in the stable yard. By the time she left twenty-two years later the boys doing Art were the mainstay of the senior school and were achieving good grades at A level Art even if they could not spell or add.

When Susan retired from teaching in 1985 she took an Open University degree in Research Methods and Statistics and set about finding out as much as possible about the connection between dyslexia and visual-spatial faculties. From this she went on to form the *The Arts Dyslexia Trust* in 1992, which she is still running today as the Society's Secretary. The aims of the Society are: *'to draw attention to the high creative potential of visually-dominant dyslexic minds and to bridge the gap between such*

minds and others who think more easily in words. It provides an advisory service for educationalists and practical help for students in art and design careers. It also aims to encourage research into the connection between dyslexia and visual-spatial faculties that can lead to exceptional ability in arts and science, and to encourage everyone to recognise and develop it for their own use and enjoyment.'

Susan's brother and sister in law sold Lodge House in the 1980s when the motorway through Kent to the Channel Tunnel was proposed and new electricity pylons, which would have spoilt the view, were due to be erected by the newly privatised electricity company. This, of course, meant that Susan had to vacate the Pottery.

Richard Parkinson
Richard worked at the Hornsey School of Art from 1960 until 1971 and became the Head of Ceramics. For a couple of years between 1966 and 1968 he also ran a Pottery in Cambridgeshire. In 1968 he moved the Pottery to London and three years later in 1971 when he stopped teaching at Hornsey he moved his Pottery yet again, this time to Wales, the home of his third wife, Dorn Williams. For the next ten years, until 1982, he ran a Pottery at Boncath near Cardigan where he decorated cast wares, such as mugs and lidded boxes with transfer print designs. His experience at Harry Davis' Crowan Pottery in Cornwall had convinced him that it was not feasible to produce hand-thrown and hand decorated tableware at an economic price. As a result he switched to decorating industrial white-ware. One of his main production lines during the 1970s and 1980s was a series of mugs which he made for the National Trust, many of which were commemoratives celebrating Royal occasions such as Charles and Diana's wedding and the birth of Prince William. His wife, Dorn Williams, designed the transfers used on the mugs. Richard died in 1985 aged 58.

Above: The rear view of a square pig, model 78, 2¼ inches long. The pig's tail forms the letter S.

INDEX

APPENDIX 1 - LIST OF MODEL NUMBERS

The following is a list of model numbers as far as they can be traced today.

Model No.	Description	Model No.	Description
1	Small bird or coptic	42	Classical head male (sold as a pair with female)
2	Lion (sold as a pair with the unicorn)	43	Classical head female
3	Unicorn	44	
4		45	
5		46	Little owl or pocket owl
6	Large cat	47	Fruit bowl
7	Money bear	48	Small cat (sold as a pair with 49)
8	Sheep		
9	Large owl	49	Small cat
10		50	Small mermaid
11		51	
12		52	Row of schoolgirls
13		53	
14		54	
15		55	
16		56	
17		57	
18		58	
19	French bulldog, Beetle	59	
20		60	Small pepper and salt
21		61	
22		62	
23	Cock	63	Oil/vinegar bottle
24	Hen	64	Cat pepper (sold as a pair with cat salt)
25			
26		65	Cat salt
27		66	
28		67	Greek head
29		68	
30		69	
31		70	Golfer
32	Chorus of birds	71	Mouse
33	Two cats	72	Cricketer
34		73	
35	Triangular dish	74	Robin
36	Large pepper and salt	75	
37		76	
38		77	
39		78	Pig, small square
40	Schoolgirl - Haystack hair (sold as a pair with Pigtails)	79	Wren
		80	Hedgehog
41	Schoolgirl - Pigtails	81	Medium plate/dish

Model No.	Description	Model No.	Description
82	Small plate/dish	121	Baby mermaid
83		122	Leaf plate
84		123	Small fish plate
85	Policeman	124	Medium fish plate
86	Barrister	125	Money pig
87	Judge	126	Long leaf dish
88		127	Bottle stopper - short hat
89		128	Bottle stopper - tall hat
90	Hand in glove	129	Bottle stopper - helmet
91	Mug half pint	130	
92	Bottle stopper - bird	131	Churchill
94		132	
95		133	
96	Bottle stopper - policeman	134	
97	Bottle stopper - diving fish	135	
98	Wide goblet III	136	
99	Squirrel	137	
100	King Canute	138	Corgi
101	Mug 1 pint	139	Boxer
102	Storage jar small	140	Peke
103	Storage jar medium	141	Poodle
104	Storage jar large	142	Little owl (flat)
105	Mustard pot	143	Square bird
106	Money cat	144	Pointing bird
107	Schoolboy	145	Nesting bird
108		146	Bird in cage
109	Cavalier	147	Peacock
110	Woman knitting	148	Small cricketer
111		149	Tennis player
112		150	Small golfer
113		151	Big owl (flat)
114		152	Coffee mug (with columns or squares)
115			
116		153	Small leaf plate
117		154	Tall goblet IV
118		155	New hedgehog
119		156	
120		157	

APPENDIX 2 - POTTERY MARKS

Not all of the Pottery marks are included here, partly because of the difficulty in reproducing very small marks, but the main reason is that they are of little help in dating pieces as many of the marks were interchangeable. However, if the word *Ltd* is used after *Richard Parkinson* the model must date from late 1954 onwards. The colour of the glaze and the number of the model are much better indicators of the date. The very early pieces were not fired to such a high level and so the body does not appear so white as later ones and the early decoration is normally a mid shade of grey. Brown decoration (red iron) also usually indicates an early piece, that is pre 1955. After 1955 the decoration tends to be either a greeny-black or black.

RICHARD PARKINSON POTTERY MARKS:

RICHARD'S SEAL:
(0.4 inches across)

IMPRESSED MARKS
(0.6 inches long)

(0.45 inches high)

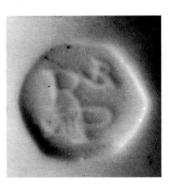

(0.5 inches long)

P for Parkinson occasionally used on very small pieces:

INK MARK
(0.6 inches high):

A variation of *Made in England* and a test mark (England is 0.25 inches long):

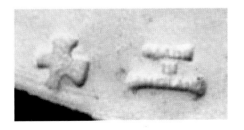

Above Left: A bronze of Barbara Johnstone, modelled by Susan in 1965. 15½ inches high. In the Johnstone family's collection.

Above Right: A bronze of Adam Johnstone, aged 2½ years, modelled by Susan in 1968. Height 9½ inches. In the Johnstone family's collection.

Left: Susan Parkinson aged 17 years, self-portrait in oils.

Above: Susan's stylised, stoneware sculpture of a dachshund, made in the early 1950s. 7½ inches high and 15 inches long.

Left: The folly designed by Susan for Michael Trevor Williams of Portmerion. 8½ inches high. In Colin's collection.

Left: Susan's terra cotta head of her grand nephew, Thomas. Made circa 1990.

Below: A terra cotta cat, 14 inches high and 16 inches long. Made by Susan in the early 1950s. The head is very similar to some of her ceramic cat models, in particular the two cats.

Above: A lion and the unicorn made for the coronation of Queen Elizabeth II and dated 1953 on the reverse. Model numbers 2 and 3, 6¾ inches high.

Below: A mural made by Susan in 1951 This is probably the very first piece made at Brabourne Lees.

Right and below: Two views of early versions of the sheep decorated with colour rather than black, which was used later. Model number 8, 6¾ inches high and 11 inches long. This style of decoration is more usual than the wax resist method used on the black and white version illustrated on page 21. The blue-grey colour was used on a number of models in the early 1950s, especially the lion and unicorn.

Bottom of page: Two wrens, model number 79, 2 inches high. The one on the left is one of the very few lustre models that Susan made in 1961.

Above: Chorus of birds, model number 32, 13 inches long and 3½ inches high.

Right: The large cat, model number 6, 14½ inches high.

Below: The nesting bird, model number 145, 2¾ inches high.

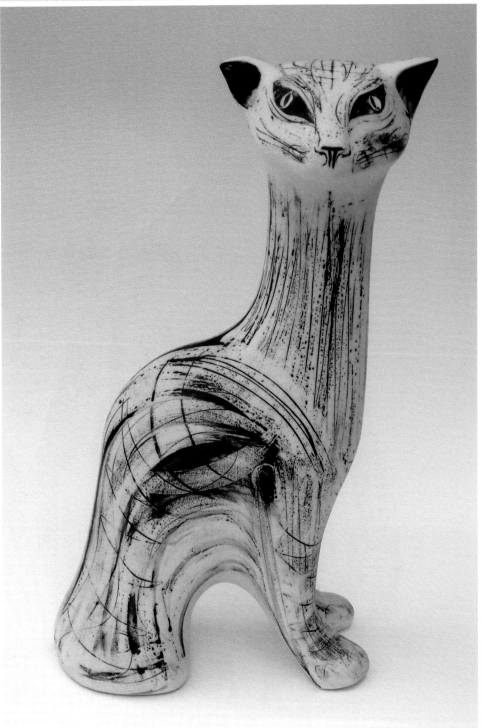

Left: Two cats, model number 33, 10 inches high. The decoration on this model is a particularly fine colour.

Below: Three piping women, 11 inches long and 8½ inches high. The decoration between models varies considerably but this one is particularly good. See the back cover for the reverse view of the piping women.

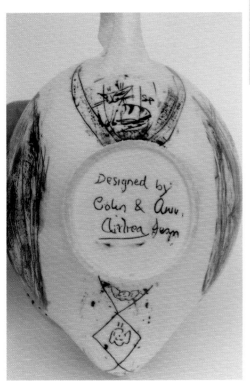

The teapot illustrated on this page is unique, but unfortunately the spout has been slightly damaged. It is 5½ inches high and was made one day for a bit of fun, probably because there was some slip left in the bucket at the end of the day. It is known as 'Nellie teapot' and, as can be seen from the base, all the workers helped to make it, including Susan who has put her initials under the handle next to the drawing of the cat. Inside the pot, on the base, is a picture of Colin's bubble car, which had no reverse gear so that it could be driven on a motorbike licence. This meant that it had to be manhandled if reverse was required! It also took all the pottery workers to the shop on occasions to buy ice creams. The teapot is in Colin's collection.

Left and below: The hand in glove, model number 90, cast from the mould formed for making rubber gloves. 14 inches tall. The design represents a tree with birds sitting on the branches formed by the fingers. This model illustrates very clearly the green tinge that the Parkinson's achieved in their glaze, which gives their models such interest.

Above: A peacock, model number 147, 3½ inches high.

Below: Two square birds, model number 143, 1¾ inches high.

Right: The large golfer, model number 70, 15 inches high.

Below: The squirrel which was in production for only a short period and was withdrawn in 1961. Model number 99, 2¾ inches high.

Bottom of the page: Two square pigs, model number 78, 2¼ inches long.

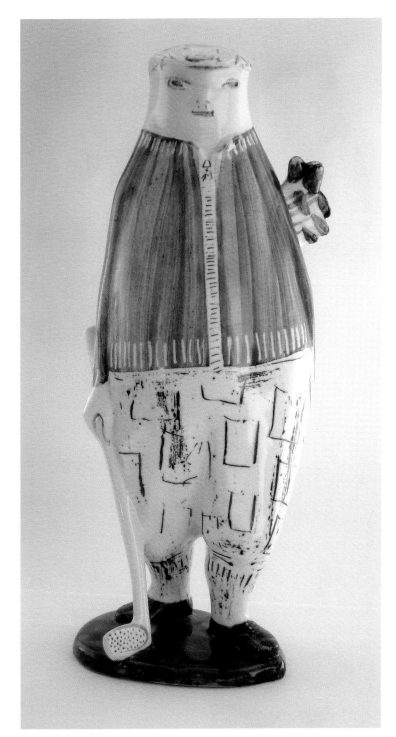

Left: A 8¾ inch plate from the chess series, with a rather unusual and menacing decoration of knights. In Colin's collection.

Below: The cover of an invitation to the preview of the 'Ceramic Texture' exhibition held at Primavera in 1955. The drawing illustrates one of Susan's stylised sculptures of a bull.

Below left: Three storage jars. Model numbers, small 102, medium 103 and large 104, 5½, 6½ and 7½ inches high.

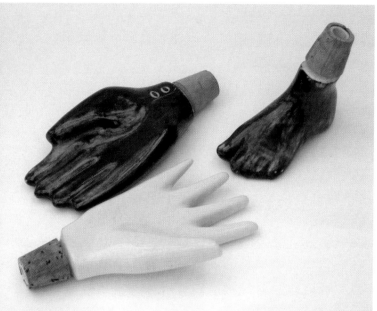

Above: One of the later models of the little owl. 2¾ inches high. In the collection of John Lejeune.

Above right: Three bottle stoppers. The open hand and closed or 'stop' hand are 5¾ inches long, including the cork. The foot is 3¼ inches in length.

Below: Two goblets and an eggcup. The right-hand goblet is tall goblet IV, model number 154, and is 4¾ inches high. The other goblet and the egg cup are 4½ inches and 2 inches high respectively.

Below right: The small golfer, model number 150, 8½ inches high.

Right: Watercolour of sheep painted by Susan.

Below: A slip-cast porcelain tile panel made by Susan in the early 1950s. 21 x 14 inches. Photograph by Clive Summerfield. The panel was made as an experiment in tile production using the slip-casting technique.

Above: A Cinque Ports Pottery money box pig, 4 inches high made circa 1963.

Above right: A Cinque Ports Pottery owl made from the large owl mould. It was made during the 1960s and has a very matt powdery finish.

Below: A Cinque Ports money box cow, 12 inches long, made circa 1963.

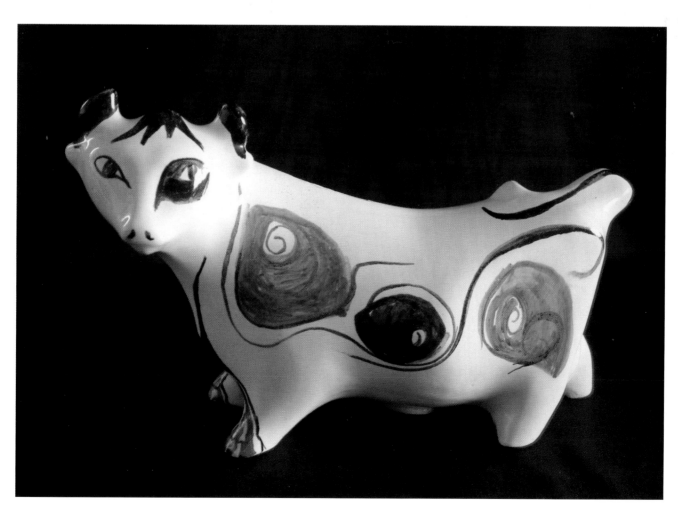

Right: The whale, one of the very few models with colour decoration. First made in 1956/57. 5½ inches long and 2½ inches high.

Below: One of Guy Neale's pictures, painted in 1954 while he was at the Pottery. Oil on board, 18 x 12 inches.

112